AN INTRODUCTION TO
Sailing

AN INTRODUCTION TO

Sailing

Peter Blake

WITH DAVID PARDON

AURUM PRESS

Copyright © Peter Blake, 1993
Copyright © David Bateman Ltd, 1993

First published in the United Kingdom by
Aurum Press Limited, 25 Bedford Avenue, London WC1B 3AT,
England, in association with
David Bateman Ltd., 'Golden Heights', 32-34 View Road,
Glenfield, Auckland, New Zealand

A CIP catalogue record for this book
is available from the British Library.

ISBN 1 85410 269 9

1998 1997 1996 1995 1994
10 9 8 7 6 5 4 3 2 1

Designed by Steve Henderson
Typeset by Typeset Graphics
Printed in Hong Kong by Colorcraft

CONTENTS

Introduction

SAILING FOR
EVERYONE

IN THOUSANDS of places all over the world, people go sailing. They range from small children nervously steering a dinghy for the first time, to grandparents and families experiencing a lifestyle that a few years ago was unknown to all but a handful of adventurers. Today there are professional blue-water racers, weekend harbour cruisers, and increasing numbers of people who, living miles from the ocean in the landlocked states of heartland USA or industrial Europe, enjoy sailing small yachts on lakes and inland waterways. And not all of them are athletic. Thanks to modern sailboat systems, even the physically handicapped can handle quite large yachts. My own country, New Zealand, now has an annual regatta for the blind.

So what attracts people to sailing? Often, far out at sea, I have asked myself, 'What am I doing here, bashing into a gale, cold, wet, tired and miserable? Why didn't I take up golf?' Such questions have come while frozen to the helm during five round-the-world yacht races, while crossing the Tasman in a trimaran with half a hull missing, while rounding Fastnet Rock in a storm that took the lives of 15 yachtsmen, sank five boats and caused another 19 to be abandoned, and even while simply making for home through a blustery sou'-westerly after a Sunday-afternoon sail.

But these were the bad times, and have been far outweighed by the good. Those schoolday afternoons at high speed in my dinghy, spinnaker set and out of control, were exhilarating beyond

Left: Why go sailing? Maybe the answer is in once-in-a-lifetime experiences such as this. The author's maxi ketch *Steinlager 2* weaves through the massive spectator fleet on Auckland's Waitemata Harbour at the start of the Auckland–Punta del Este leg of the 1989-90 Whitbread Round the World Race. *Photo: Group Kiwi.*

Right: . . . or maybe it's in the excitement and action of dinghy racing, whether the friendly, family atmosphere of club competition or the fierce, international world of high-tech classes such as these Olympic 470s. *Photo: Roger Lean-Vercoe.*

description. Surfing a maxi through the Southern Ocean at 35 knots in 12-m (40-ft) seas with no help on hand should anything go wrong, was an experience no one could ever forget. And no words could express the feeling of pride, achievement and comradeship on that day in May 1990 when we brought *Steinlager 2* into Southampton Dock, having won the Whitbread Round the World Race by just 36 minutes, a bare 8 km (5 miles) ahead of fellow New Zealanders Grant Dalton and the crew of *Fisher and Paykel* after 53,100 km (33,000 miles) of virtual boat-for-boat racing. That high point in my life of sailing wiped away all those moments of despair, discomfort, danger and fear, and, for me, has answered the question, 'Why go sailing?'

Sailing offers everything: physical exercise, mental recreation and a chance to relax away from the crowds, the traffic and the pressures of modern life, even while no further from all those things than on a harbour or lake within sight and sound of the city skyscrapers. It does more than sooth the mind and soul, however. It challenges. It requires skill, full use of the senses, awareness and respect for the environment, and, above all, self-reliance and the ability to work as a team. Unique among sports and pastimes, sailing can be enjoyed in almost limitless forms, in a variety of boats, alone or with others, far out to sea or on a pond in a crowded city park. It can be, as it is for me, a complete way of life, or it can occupy no more than an hour or two on summer weekends or annual vacations. Above all, it is something all members of all families, young and old, large or small, can take part in, separately and together. It can be enjoyed noisily in a crowd by energetic athletes, or quietly alone by introspective dreamers.

So how does one become a yachtsman or yachtswoman, able to appreciate all these

Sailing is for all people of all ages, enjoyable separately or together and in limitless forms, from high-tech competitive ocean-racing *(left)* to leisurely cruising *(above)*, or even, as Rat observed in Kenneth Grahame's *Wind In The Willows*, 'simply messing about in boats'. *Photos: Rainbow Charters/Roger Lean-Vercoe.*

wonderful sensations? What do you need and how do you begin?

Someone who has never been on a tennis court can't just pick up a racquet and start playing. Merely by putting on a pair of boots one cannot become an instant mountaineer. Most people at some stage have taken hold of a golf club, only to discover how maddeningly difficult it is just to hit the ball, let alone hit it in a straight line! All sports take time to learn, call for certain disciplines, and are invariably harder than they appear to those who have never taken them up.

Yachting is unusual in that, despite involving more equipment and technology, and having spawned more complex terminology than any other recreational activity, it is, in its basic form, easy to pick up. New Zealander Harold Bennett, who has coached Olympic and America's Cup yachting teams, and who is universally recognised as one of the world's finest sailing instructors, tells

how seven- and eight-year-olds climb into a
dinghy, their first time in a boat of any kind, and,
with someone aboard to show them the basics,
sail it back to the beach or lakeside at the end
of their first lesson. The dynamics of wind-power,
and the mechanics of harnessing that power with
a sail and controlling it with a rudder, can be
explained in complicated scientific language and
mathematical formulae. It is the source of endless
research, using the most advanced computers —
but it can also be presented in simple words and
everyday language.

In the pages which follow I'll talk about how
a sailboat moves and explain how to control those
movements. I'll look at some of the different
types of sailboat, how they are built and the way
in which they are designed to carry out particular
functions. But this is a book about the practice
rather than the theory of sailboats and sailing,
so while it will touch on racing to win as well
as cruising for fun, on small dinghies and ocean
maxis, on monohulls and multihulls, on the

Left: Even a relatively small dinghy can offer the whole family (not forgetting 'Fido') relaxation, adventure and a new outlook on favourite and familiar places. And you don't have to worry about finding somewhere to park or running out of gas. *Photo: Roger Lean-Vercoe.*

Above: There's more to sailing than can be found in the boat itself, and many ways of enjoying the pleasures of the sea and inland waterways. *Photo: Rainbow Charters.*

Right: Sailing the Peter Blake way — skipper Blake *(right)* and crew keep an eye out for the opposition, far astern of *Steinlager 2* as the Whitbread maxi powers hard to windward. *Photo: Boating World.*

equipment of sailboats, their maintenance and safety, on boat handling and navigation, it will all be in terms which can be readily understood without having to reach for a sailing dictionary. The aim is to whet the reader's appetite for, and increase the understanding of, the sport that is my life and which gives me, and millions of others, so much pleasure. After that, it is simply a matter of expanding this basic understanding and developing your knowledge to whatever extent gives you the maximum personal satisfaction.

This book is a dip into the knowledge and experience I have gained from a lifetime packed with sailing in virtually all its forms and in all types of boat. I believe it has something for everyone. I hope it helps and encourages those with no knowledge at all to sample the pleasures of sailing, while for those already sailing it may suggest some new ideas and different points of view.

Peter Blake

Above: Despite complex equipment and technology, the basics of sailing are easily learned. After only a few lessons, even small children become confident and proficient handlers of dinghies such as the Optimist and Mirror. *Photo: Roger Lean-Vercoe.*

Right: Endless practical and theoretical research, including hours of computer time, go into understanding the dynamics of wind-power and harnessing it for maximum efficiency, but the way in which the wind drives a sailboat can also be presented in simple terms and everyday language. *Photo: Roger Lean-Vercoe.*

Chapter 1

WHEN THE
WIND BLOWS

NO SUBJECT is closer to a sailor's heart than the weather, an unknown, uncontrollable factor creating both the appeal and the challenge of sailing and setting it apart from other recreational activities. Weather changes from friend to foe in an instant, and while neither instinct nor science can forecast those changes with total certainty, he is a foolish yachtsman who does not constantly seek to improve his knowledge of the elements. There is no short-cut to, or substitute for, experience, and one of the strongest tributes paid to any racing sailor is that he 'picks the shifts'. Races are won by skippers who, blending skill with instinct, are marginally ahead of the opposition in detecting a coming change in wind strength or direction, i.e., in picking the shift.

The science of meteorology is fascinating and complex, but the most advanced electronic systems and equipment are no substitute for knowing the area in which you are sailing. Likewise, familiarity with, and constant monitoring of, your yacht's instruments, attention to weather forecasts and the wonders of Weatherfax can do much to reduce the chances of being caught with the wrong sails or in the wrong position on the racetrack when conditions change, but there is still much that comes naturally to the experienced sailor.

Weather changes from friend to foe in an instant — and you don't have to be actually sailing to learn what a dangerous enemy it can be. These yachts were in what their owners believed to be sheltered anchorages when a storm swept across Concarneau on the coast of Brittany, France. *Photo: See And Sea.*

Picking the shifts

The old square-rigger sailing crews had endless sayings and rhymes on which to base their weather forecasting in the days before electronics, and a few are still worth remembering. They form the background against which many of the world's best yachtsmen have developed their skill at picking the shifts.

Red sky at night, shepherds' delight

A red sky is the reflection of the setting sun on high cloud formations usually associated with high-pressure systems, or 'highs' as they are known. It usually foretells fair weather but should

Left: Races are won by skippers who, blending skill with instinct, are marginally ahead of the opposition in detecting coming changes in wind strength and/or direction. *Photo: Roger Lean-Vercoe.*

Above: All-action 5.5-m (18-ft) skiffs, their four- or five-person crews hiked far out to windward on tubular frames, are an exciting feature of the Australian sailing scene. Large sums of money are regularly wagered with bookmakers, who use fast powerboats to follow the race fleets. *Photo: Boating World.*

Right: Brooding skies and a pounding sea — not all racing takes place in idyllic breezes under an azure-blue heaven. *Photo: Roger Lean-Vercoe.*

Overleaf: Keeping an eye on the sky as well as on the yacht's instruments and sails, Dawn Riley concentrates on holding a course to windward while her crew stack the windward rail. *Photo: Roger Lean-Vercoe.*

be treated with caution as fine weather does not necessarily mean light winds.

Red sky in the morning, sailors take warning
A red morning sky is the reflection of the rising sun off much lower altitude clouds associated with low-pressure systems ('lows' or 'troughs'). As these are more compact than highs, you can more reliably expect the weather to deteriorate rapidly over the next few hours.

Wind before rain, the sun will shine again
Freshening wind before rain generally means a short-lived squall, following which conditions will revert to what they were before. (This adage works well!)

Rain before wind, take tops'ls in
Rain before an increase in wind means a change for the worse. The wind will usually increase quickly soon after the rain starts and remain strong after it stops.

If visibility is extremely good, the weather is unlikely to remain settled for long. Conversely, a fine-weather haze usually suggests good weather for several more days.

Always keep a close watch on other yachts in your region of water. Carry good binoculars and use them whenever you can't see easily with the naked eye. Never stop looking around — it's amazing what you learn from simple observation. Use signs on land as well as water for a better appreciation of what is going on around you. On light days, for example, smoke from on-shore chimneys and bonfires is a good indicator of wind direction.

Make full use of weather forecasts, listening carefully and writing down anything relative to your area and the general situation. If your yacht is larger than a dinghy, carry a good barometer and keep a sharp eye on it, especially if the sky looks ominous or the forecast is for deteriorating conditions. A fast drop in millibars is invariably accompanied by a 'front'. A change in wind

Left: When anchored, make sure you have enough room to swing full circle to the extent of the anchor warp without touching bottom — not so easy when the anchorage is as popular as Port Fitzroy on New Zealand's Great Barrier Island, pictured during the holiday season. *Photo: Group Kiwi.*

Right: One of the most familiar of weather tell-tales: a setting sun reflecting off high cloud produces the traditional ''red sky at night'' that invariably means fair (though not necessarily calm) weather ahead. *Photo: Roger Lean-Vercoe.*

Below: A rainbow heralds the imminent onslaught of a harbour squall. *Photo: Group Kiwi.*

direction and rise in the barometer reading will follow as the front passes over.

If anchored snugly for the night with the wind blowing strongly, be sure to check what will happen when the front passes in the middle of the night and the wind switches direction. Will you have enough room to swing at anchor or are you going to be totally exposed and possibly even washed ashore?

All sailors should be familiar with Admiral Beaufort's Scale of Wind Speeds as used by marine-weather forecasters throughout the world. It ranges from Number 0 (calm, less than 1 knot) to Number 10 (storm, or whole gale, 48–55 knots). Generally speaking, Beaufort Force 5 (fresh breeze, 17–21 knots) is about the limit for the average dinghy, while prudent keelboat skippers start looking for shelter at Force 6 (strong breeze, 22–27 knots). Forces 9 (strong gale, 41–47 knots) and 10 are survival conditions for any sailboat.

Tidal influences

The other major influence on sailing conditions is, of course, the tide. It is one of the most important factors to be considered when making a passage that takes you round a headland or cape where tides run more strongly than in open water.

Tidal ranges (i.e., differences in height between high and low water) are essential information. In the Golfe de St Malo on the northwest coast of France, for example, a 12.19-m (40-ft) rise and fall is common, and at Mont St Michel the tide rises so quickly over the flat, sandy bottom that it can overtake a galloping horse. On the other hand, Caribbean and Mediterranean tidal ranges are no more than a metre or so. Whatever the range, you need to take it into consideration when navigating and, of course, when anchoring. I'm certainly not the only yachtsman who has had the frightening experience of waking at night from a steeply-angled bunk to find the keel and rudder lodged dangerously among rocks.

While listening carefully to weather forecasts, referring to up-to-date charts and carrying all the right equipment, it is still useful to ask someone

Right: Close inshore the effect of wind can be severely distorted by surrounding hills . . . beware of getting too close and losing the wind altogether. *Photo: Group Kiwi.*

Beaufort Wind Scale A table recording the velocity of winds and their speeds.

Beaufort Number	Description	Speed in knots*	Height of sea†	Deep sea criteria
0	Calm	less than 1	—	Sea mirror-smooth.
1	Light air	1-3	0.07m (¼ft)	Small wavelets like scales, no crests.
2	Light breeze	4-6	0.15m (½ft)	Small wavelets still short but more pronounced. Crests glassy and do not break.
3	Gentle breeze	7-10	0.60m (2ft)	Large wavelets. Crests begin to break. Foam is glassy.
4	Moderate breeze	11-16	1.06m (3½ft)	Small waves becoming longer; more frequent white horses.
5	Fresh breeze	17-21	1.82m (6ft)	Moderate waves, and longer; many white horses.
6	Strong breeze	22-27	2.89m (9½ft)	Large waves begin to form; white crests more extensive.
7	Near gale	28-33	4.11m (13½ft)	Sea heaps up; white foam blown in streaks.
8	Gale	34-40	5.48m (18ft)	Moderately high waves of greater length; crests begin to form spindrift. Foam blown in well-marked streaks.
9	Strong gale	41-47	7.01m (23ft)	High waves; dense streaks of foam. Crests begin to roll over.
10	Storm	48-55	8.83m (29ft)	Very high waves with long, overhanging crests. Surface of sea becomes white with great patches of foam. Visibility affected.
11	Violent storm	56-63	11.27m (37ft)	Exceptionally high waves. Sea completely covered with foam.
	Hurricane	64+		The air is filled with spray and visibility seriously affected.

*Measured at the height of 10m above sea-level. †In the open sea remote from land.

Previous page: There is no shortage of wind for competitors in this McNamara Bowl race, an event for all-women crews. *Photo: Roger Lean-Vercoe.*

Left: 'Keep an eye on the sky and never stop looking around; it's amazing what you learn from simple observation.' *Photo: Boating World.*

Below: Eddies and currents in protected waters such as these yachts are racing in can be of tremendous help to both the racing and the cruising yacht. Look out for bands of foam or changes in water colour that mark the tide-lines. *Photo: Group Kiwi.*

Right: Well offshore and with a stiff breeze blowing, it's all very different, as French yachtswoman Florence Arthaud enjoys an armchair ride atop the weather hull of the trimaran *Pierre 1er. Photo: Roger Lean-Vercoe.*

who has firsthand knowledge of the area you plan to sail in whether they have experienced any peculiar weather or tidal conditions, or if they have any hints on anchorages that may look good on the chart but in fact are untenable because of a huge swell that rolls around the headland, etc.

Wind effect distortion

In harbours and protected waters where most dinghy sailing takes place, the effect of wind can be severely distorted by surrounding hills and even buildings. In a racing situation, this local knowledge can mean the difference between winning and losing, no matter what the size of yacht. The same applies to currents and tides. Many strong currents have back eddies which run close to the shore and can be of tremendous help to both the racing and cruising yacht. In harbours, look out for tide-lines — bands of foam or differently-coloured water.

If you are beating to windward and the surrounding land is not particularly high, stay close to the windward shore. Wind alters in direction as it comes off the land, so instead of beating you can often find yourself laying straight through. Apart from this, the sea will be calmer closer inshore. If the windward shore is cliff-lined, however, beware of getting in too close and losing the wind altogether.

Summary

• Listen to the weather forecast and write it down. Remember that most meteorological stations are ashore and they are therefore recording wind speeds over land. Allow for an increase of anything up to 10 knots in the wind speed at sea.

• Plan your trip. Know when the tide is high and low and what the range is.

• Be sure to have an up-to-date chart of the area in which you are sailing and know the meaning of all the chart symbols.

• When anchored, make sure you have enough room to swing in a full circle to the extent of the anchor warp and without touching bottom.

• Keep an eye on the sky. Remember the

rhymes and what they mean.
*   If possible, cut the latest weather map from a local newspaper and use it to make your own forecasts.
*   Watch the barometer and learn what the changes and rate of change signify.
*   If a change is forecast, or your own reading of the signs suggests a change, plan what you are going to do beforehand. You will have enough to worry about in driving rain, howling wind and poor visibility without trying to remember where you put the chart and/or tide tables.
*   Learn to recognise the land signs as well as those at sea.
*   When beating to windward, keep towards the windward shore where possible — you'll have a faster, easier journey.

If beating to windward, stay towards the windward shore wherever possible . . . you'll have a faster, easier, more comfortable journey. *Photo: Roger Lean-Vercoe.*

Chapter 2

HARNESSING
THE WIND

ALTHOUGH sailboats have been designed and built in countless shapes and sizes and for many purposes, from the Roman merchant ships of A.D. 200 to modern racing yachts, and from 1.8-m (6-ft) dinghies with a single sail to the likes of the *Thomas W. Lawson*, 116-m (383-ft) long with seven masts and 25 sails, we are looking at them purely as pleasure craft in the shape of either dinghies or keelboats, monohulls or multihulls.

Dinghies are small (up to about 4.3-m (14-ft)) one- or two-person boats with a centreboard that can be pushed down into the water and pulled up again when necessary. Larger sailboats occasionally have a centreboard, but most have

a fixed keel bolted to the bottom of the boat. The keel is weighted with a measured amount of ballast, generally lead or iron. Monohulls and multihulls are self-explanatory ... one hull (*monohull*), two or three hulls (*multihull*), described more specifically as *catamaran* and *trimaran* respectively.

The driving force
It needs no deep scientific understanding to recognise that if you stand a mast and sail in a rowing-boat, canoe or any other kind of vessel lacking a keel or centreboard, the boat will fall over as soon as the wind hits the sail. A sailboat

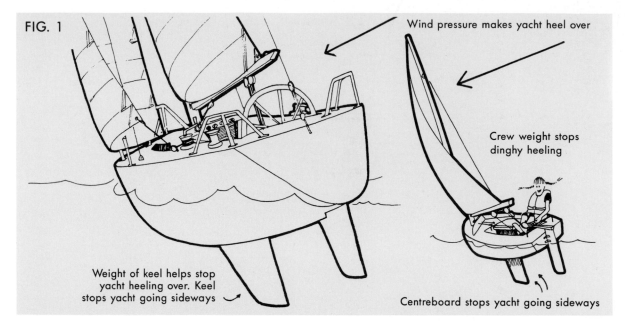

FIG. 1

Wind pressure makes yacht heel over

Crew weight stops dinghy heeling

Weight of keel helps stop yacht heeling over. Keel stops yacht going sideways

Centreboard stops yacht going sideways

counters this wind pressure with a righting force, or lever. In a keelboat the righting force (called **righting moment**) is provided by the ballast in the keel. In a centreboard dinghy it comes from the crew ('live' ballast) sitting on the windward side of the hull, or even stretched out on a trapeze. In both cases the keel or centreboard also prevents the wind simply pushing the vessel sideways through the water (Fig. 1).

With the boat held upright, or nearly upright, and unable to be pushed sideways, the wind is deflected either side of the sail. This generates high and low pressure areas, depending on the shape of the sail and angle at which it is set, and these pressures create a driving force which moves the hull through the water. Combinations of sail and rudder angle will drive the yacht in any required direction other than to within about 45 degrees either side of that from which the wind is blowing.

The direction in which a yacht is sailed relative to the direction from which the wind is blowing, is called the **point of sail** (Fig. 2), and being completely familiar with these points of sail is as basic to being able to sail as knowing how to cope with straight roads and corners is to driving a car. Let's begin by describing the points of sail in simple terms.

Right: The smile of satisfaction that comes with knowing you have mastered wind and water. Linda Andersen shows the enjoyment that came with winning the Europe Class Gold Medal at the 1992 Olympic Games in Barcelona. *Photo: Roger Lean-Vercoe.*

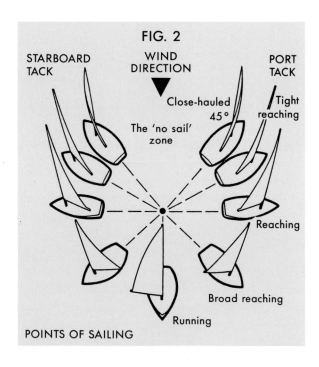

FIG. 2

STARBOARD TACK

WIND DIRECTION

PORT TACK

Close-hauled 45°

Tight reaching

The 'no sail' zone

Reaching

Broad reaching

Running

POINTS OF SAILING

Points of sail

With the wind from ahead

As already stated, no sailboat can move directly into the wind or even closer to it than about 45 degrees, so if your destination is within this 90-degree arc, you have to get there by zigzagging from one side to the other of the straight-line course. This is called *tacking*, sailing **on the wind**, or *beating*, and part of the skill of the experienced sailor is in judging just how long each tack should be in order for the boat to reach its destination in the shortest possible time.

With the wind from the side

If the direction in which you want to sail means the wind is blowing from a point within an arc approximately 45 degrees forward to 45 degrees rearward (aft) of the vessel's centreline, you will be *reaching*. With the wind near the forward limit of that arc, you are *close-reaching*, *tight reaching* or *close-hauled*. As it moves towards

Left and above: The righting force, or leverage, with which a centreboard dinghy counters the wind pressure on its sails, is provided by the crew ('live' ballast) sitting on the windward side of the hull, or even stretched out on a trapeze. While the larger keelboat gains its righting force from the ballast (usually lead) in its keel, it, too, will benefit from a few helping hands (and bodies) on the windward rail. *Photos: Boating World/Nathan Bilow.*

Right: Zigzagging, or beating, into the wind, the yacht just visible in the foreground on port tack barely squeezes between the pair on starboard tack. International Regulations for Preventing Collisions at Sea require the vessel on port tack to keep clear of a vessel, or vessels, on starboard tack. *Photo: Group Kiwi.*

midway, i.e., 90 degrees to the vessel's centreline, you are on a **beam reach**, and as it moves towards the rearward (aft) end of the arc you are **broad reaching**.

With the wind from behind

If the wind is coming from within the arc approximately 45 degrees rearward (aft) either side of the vessel's centreline, you are **running**, or sailing **off the wind**. A sailboat moving with the wind from immediately behind is often described as being on a **dead run** or **flat off**.

From beat to reach to run

A sailboat is moved from one point of sail to another by its wheel or tiller, and it's important to remember here that while a tiller must be moved in the opposite direction to that in which you want to go, a wheel is geared in the same way as a car, i.e., to turn the boat in the direction in which the wheel is rotated.

It's also worth noting here that, unlike a car, a sailboat generates momentum through the water (called **carrying way**) which means it will not respond instantly when the tiller or wheel is turned. There will be a delay dependent on several factors (the boat's speed, size, shape, also condition of the water, etc.) and the effect is likely to be more pronounced on a wheel-steered vessel than on one using a tiller.

Trimming the sail

The tiller or wheel will turn the boat into the direction in which you want to travel (your **course**), but you will also have to trim the sail if you don't want to just stand still, sail backwards or, even worse, capsize!

Let's look again at the different points of sail and see what happens to the wind as it flows over the sail, and why the sail must be trimmed. Fig. 3 illustrates a sailboat on a course as close to the wind as possible (i.e., 45 degrees, or close-hauled). The wind comprises billions of particles of air, but we are looking at just two of these particles

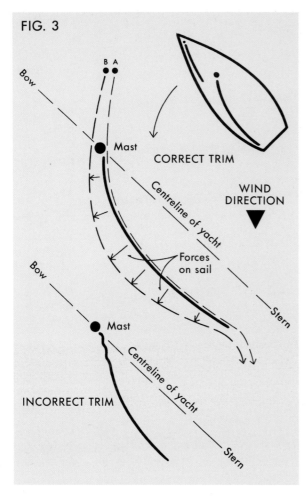

FIG. 3

CORRECT TRIM

WIND DIRECTION ▼

Bow

B A

Mast

Centreline of yacht

Forces on sail

Stern

Bow

Mast

Centreline of yacht

INCORRECT TRIM

Stern

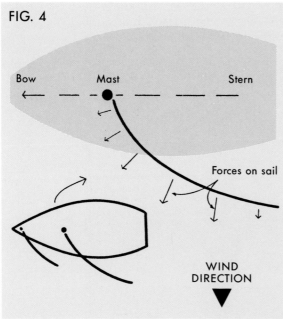

FIG. 4

Bow   Mast   Stern

Forces on sail

WIND DIRECTION ▼

(A and B), arriving at the mast together, but on different sides. Even though they are extremely small, these air particles have a mass (i.e., they weigh something), and just as a golf club has a force exerted on it by the ball as the two make contact, so particle A, travelling on the sail's windward side, exerts a force on the sail as it makes contact.

Particle B, however, is being deflected away from the sail by the latter's outward curve, and this is creating a vacuum on the back, or *lee* side, of the sail. The net result is pressure, most of which is trying to force the sail sideways. But because the sail is aerofoil-shaped like the wing of an aeroplane, some of this pressure is in a forward direction. Thus a puff of wind comprising billions of these tiny particles of air is having two effects: it is causing the sailboat to *heel* (lean over) and to move forward.

As you use the rudder to shift the boat's direction further away from the wind (i.e., onto a reach), most of the wind's force on the sail begins pushing the boat forward and only a small amount is pushing sideways and trying to capsize it. This is one reason why reaching is the easiest point of sailing (Fig. 4).

Now, move even further away from the wind so that it comes from behind the boat and you are running, then all the wind pressure is forcing you forward. The logical conclusion from this is that running with the wind directly behind is the fastest point of sail, but in fact this is not so because as water resistance builds up and drags along the sides of the hull, the boat may in fact lose speed. Some sailboat designs will therefore be at their fastest on a reach.

Sailing from scratch

Now let's go back to the point where you are sitting in the cockpit (wearing a lifejacket, of course) and waiting to move off. With the *mainsheet* (i.e., the rope attached to the sail) loose, the sail will simply flap in the wind and the boat will bob around without moving in any particular direction. As you pull the mainsheet in (called *hardening in*), the sails begin to 'go to sleep', the flapping decreases and the boat begins to move forward. The closer to the wind you want to sail, the further in you will have to trim the sail; close-hauled, it will be almost parallel to the boat's centreline.

When you move onto a reach you will need to ease the mainsheet and allow the sail to move further out on the side opposite to that from which the wind is blowing (Fig. 5). How far out you need to trim the sail for the boat to reach its fastest or most comfortable speed is a matter of constant assessment and adjustment. Trimming the sail for optimum efficiency is the real art of sailing and my advice to beginners is to always ease the sail out as far as possible until it starts to flap or lift. This applies to all sails — mainsails, headsails, genoas and, in most cases, spinnakers, though in heavy weather there are exceptions to the rule, which we discuss later.

The broach

Running off the wind, your sail will be eased out approximately 90 degrees to the vessel's centreline. But when easing out the sail in strong winds, beware the sailor's nightmare — the *broach*!

Assume you are running with the wind from *astern* (behind) and the sail out to *starboard* (i.e. right-hand side looking forward). Should you allow the boat to wander to one side, or should the wind suddenly shift a degree or so, some of the previously mentioned particles of air could slip round in front of the sail and cause it to slam from one side to the other, in this case from starboard to *port* (right to left). This is the *uncontrolled*, or *crash gybe*, and apart from the danger of you being knocked out, overboard, or both, by the swinging boom, the violence of the shift could break the mast. In any case your boat will almost certainly *broach*, i.e., turn *beam-on* (side-on) to the wind and sea, at which point you may find yourself on your ear with mast and sail in the water.

The crash-gybe can happen to the most experienced crews and on the biggest ocean yachts

Above: Beginners should always ease the sail out as far as possible, as this young Optimist skipper is learning from her coach alongside. *Photo: Roger Lean-Vercoe.*

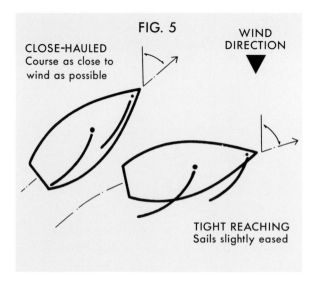

FIG. 5

WIND DIRECTION

CLOSE-HAULED
Course as close to wind as possible

TIGHT REACHING
Sails slightly eased

Above: Sailing in its simplest form. A young Topper crewman hauls on the mainsheet to trim the sail for maximum efficiency, while his skipper uses the tiller to hold the boat on course. *Photo: Roger Lean-Vercoe.*

Right: With the wind from directly aft, Round-the-World racer *Yamaha* is on a run, or sailing flat off with spinnaker set and mainsail almost square. *Photo: Boating World.*

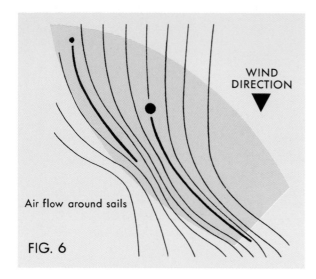

Air flow around sails

FIG. 6

WIND
DIRECTION
▼

head, of the spinnaker is attached by a *halyard* to the mast, one bottom corner to the spinnaker boom set to windward, and the other corner to the spinnaker sheet.

A real racing buff's sail, the spinnaker is probably the most difficult of all to trim and control, especially as it is so large and the unfortunate crew have to work on it from the 'sharp end', or narrowest part of the deck. A slight drop in strength or change of direction in the wind and it will collapse — usually in front of the boat where, unless the crew are very quick, it will be progressively dragged further and further under the hull, much to the embarrassment and consternation of all on board and the hilarity of onlookers and opposition.

Right: 'Telltales', or short lengths of knitting wool attached just in from the luff (front edge) of the sail of this Optimist, indicate whether the flow of air over the sail is smooth or turbulent. *Photo: Boating World.*

Below: The Whitbread maxi, *Fisher and Paykel*, shows off the massive amount of sail that can be carried on a ketch, i.e., mainmast ahead of the shorter mizzen mast. *Photo: Group Kiwi.*

and is something to which the helmsman must be constantly alert when sailing off the wind, particularly in stronger breezes.

Auxiliary sails

So far we have considered only one sail, the mainsail, but, while many dinghies — particularly beginner's classes such as the Optimist — carry only one sail, most racing dinghies as well as all larger craft are rigged for two, three or more sails. Some larger keelboats have more than one mast and, rigged as a *ketch, schooner* or *yawl*, will carry proportionately more sail.

The basic second, or auxiliary, sail is the *headsail*, set forward of the mast and attached to the *forestay*. On most *sloop-rigged* (i.e., one-masted) dinghies and keelboats, this is a single sail called a *jib*, but a *cutter-rigged* vessel will fly a second headsail, called a *staysail*, behind the jib. Today's keelboats use a large headsail called a *genoa*, which overlaps the mainsail and is set in light to fresh winds when sailing close-hauled or broad reaching.

Briefly, the function of the headsail is to clean up the air-flow around the back of the mainsail, producing a more efficient combination (Fig. 6).

The *spinnaker*, often brightly coloured and patterned, is a three-sided sail set at the very front of the vessel when reaching or running and when the mainsail and jib are eased out. The top, or

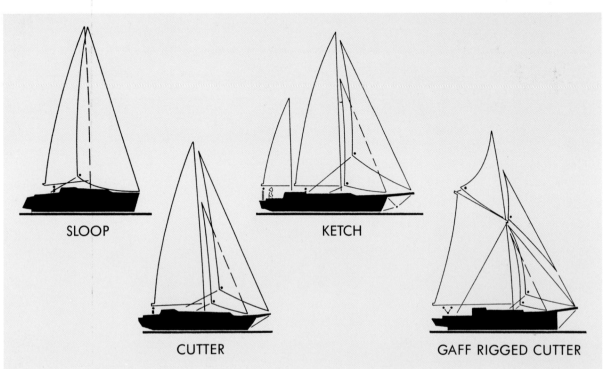

SLOOP

CUTTER

KETCH

GAFF RIGGED CUTTER

Left: A Soling crew midway through a downwind gybe, moving the sails from one side to the other — a tricky manoeuvre, especially for the for'ard hand who has to swing the spinnaker and its pole from one side of the mast to the other while attempting to keep it full and drawing. *Photo: Roger Lean-Vercoe.*

Above: Maiden approaching the Punta del Este finish line in the 1989/90 Whitbread Round the World Race. *Photo: Roger Lean-Vercoe.*

Apparent wind

We have now talked in simple terms about the sailboat's source of power, i.e., the wind in its sails, but so far we have considered the wind only in terms of its *true* direction and speed. What often confuses the novice sailor, but which has to be recognised and coped with, is the *apparent* wind caused by the motion of the boat through the water.

If you stand holding a flag in a wind of, say, 2 knots, the flag just begins to flow. Run into the wind and the flag streams out behind. That is because the apparent wind affecting the flag is the true wind speed plus the speed at which you are running. Turn and run *with* the wind and the reverse applies, i.e., the flag is affected by the true wind speed *minus* the speed at which you are running. This apparent wind will also vary in direction from its true direction depending on your point of sailing (Fig. 7).

On large craft, vector diagrams or electronic instruments are used to assess apparent wind speed and direction and relay them to the helmsman, but for the beginner and small-dinghy sailor, probably the simplest aid to sail trim is the

The spinnaker is attached by a halyard to the mast and to the spinnaker boom set to windward. For the crew, it often calls for acrobatics at the 'sharp end'.
Photo: Franco Pace (Agence DPPI).

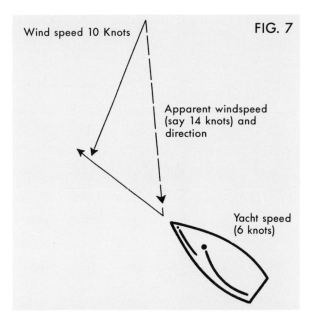

FIG. 7

Wind speed 10 Knots

Apparent windspeed (say 14 knots) and direction

Yacht speed (6 knots)

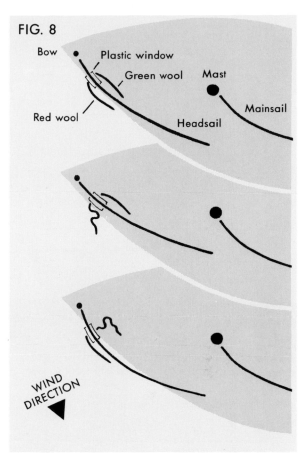

FIG. 8

Bow

Plastic window

Green wool

Mast

Red wool

Mainsail

Headsail

WIND DIRECTION

Left: A telltale, or ''wool'', streams from the leech of this 420 class dinghy being sailed hard to windward by Princess Anne, with Kate Rogers on the trapeze. *Photo: Roger Lean-Vercoe.*

Below: On larger keelboats, electronic instruments assess apparent wind speed and direction and relay them to the helmsman. *Photo: Group Kiwi.*

telltale, or *wool,* attached to the sail. Telltales are short lengths of knitting wool, about 7.5cm (3in.), attached about 38cm (15in.) in from the *luff* (front edge) and *leech* (back edge) of the sail. These indicate whether the flow of air over the sail is smooth (*laminar*) or turbulent, which means the sail is stalled and not driving the boat (Fig. 8).

The use of different coloured wool for port and starboard, along with clear plastic windows sewn into the sail, makes for easier sail trimming.

Summary

• Learn the Points of Sail, i.e., the direction in which a yacht moves relative to the direction from which the wind is blowing.
• Trim sail(s) to maintain forward momentum.
• Stay alert to avoid the risk of a crash-gybe or broach.
• Apparent wind is created by forward movement of the boat.

Chapter 3

THE RIGHT
BOAT FOR YOU

WHATEVER your choice of sailboat, a dinghy on the local lake, family trailer-yacht on the sound or harbour, or serious blue-water racer, you will be investing a lot of money. For most people a boat is their third most valuable asset after a home and car; for some it will be even more valuable than the car. For this reason, as well as for the prime considerations of safety and satisfaction, buying a boat needs careful thought and as much help and advice as is available.

In terms of cost and size, the decision process is not unlike buying a house or car, but from that point the three have little in common. Indeed, the risk of making an unwise choice is probably greater with a boat than with either a house or car. So let's look first at the factors governing

which type of boat is most likely to suit your needs, and in the next chapter we can talk about some of the points to be considered when buying secondhand.

It's important to remember that the pleasure of boating, even the safety of you and your family, can be jeopardised by choosing the wrong boat. Buy a car that is too small or too big for your needs, that is underpowered or an expensive gas-guzzler, and you still have something that will get you from A to B and perform its other essential functions. Buy a yacht that is too tender, needs four gorillas on the rail in 10 knots of wind, is too heavy for your car to tow, is wet from stem to stern on every point of sail and has 154 cm of head room in which your 164 cm has to stand,

Above: Blue sky, blue sea and friends to relax with . . . it looks idyllic, and it is. But choose the wrong boat and the safety of your family and friends could be at risk. *Photo: Rainbow Charters.*

Right: For thousands of young people around the world, boardsailing has been the boom watersport of the past decade. These two are enjoying a fair breeze on Lake Pupuke in Auckland, New Zealand. *Photo: Group Kiwi.*

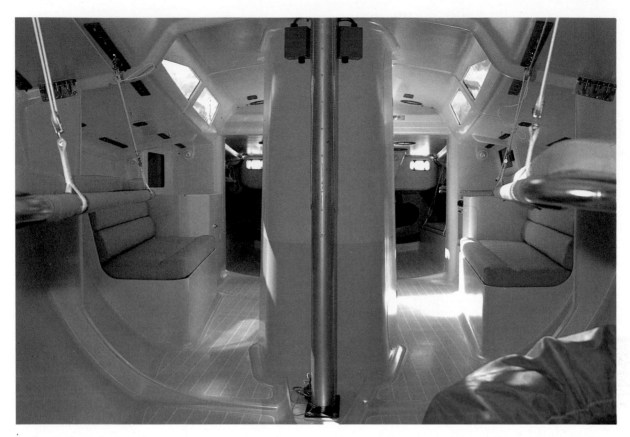

and you have invested in misery. A stripped-out flyer with enough sail area to win the America's Cup, but a plastic bucket to meet the calls of nature, might do something for your ego, but will not contribute much towards domestic harmony.

Points for early consideration

1. If your boating activities are to be strictly of the family cruising type, do you in fact want a sailboat or would you be better served by a powerboat? That may sound like treason in a book about sailing, but a lot of people, attracted by the romantic image of billowing sails, rattling halyards and fickle winds, soon lose interest on finding that they can't get where they want to go just by changing gears and turning a wheel. The cruising sailor's enjoyment is in the old adage that it is better to travel than to arrive. Make sure you, your family and everyone else likely to be involved are therefore committed to sailing and prepared to spend the time and effort it demands in return for its pleasures and sense of fulfilment.

Above: The clean, efficient interior of *Ice Fire*, a high-tech Sydney-Hobart racer designed by New Zealander Alan Mummery with few concessions to home comfort. Contrast this with the interior *(above right)* of a cruising-oriented Oceanis 400 by Beneteau. *Photos: Group Kiwi/Boating World.*

Right: There's much to be said for taking life easy and just following the wind, but many newcomers to sailing lose interest when they find that progress can be slow and they can't get anywhere just by changing gears and turning a wheel. For them, a powerboat might be the wiser option. *Photo: Rainbow Charters.*

Left: If the budget doesn't run to a super-yacht, why not something like this lovely old cruiser, seen here off the Spanish coast. *Photo: Roger Lean-Vercoe.*

Above: With its characteristic pram bow and solid wood construction, the 3-m (10-ft) traditional-looking Mirror has grown steadily in popularity over the years and, despite its relatively heavy weight, is an excellent little sailboat. *Photo: Roger Lean-Vercoe.*

Right: The 2.13-m (7-ft) Optimist is popular the world over as a safe, stable, easily-to-sail dinghy for youngsters. *Photo: Roger Lean-Vercoe.*

Right, so you definitely want a sailboat.

2. What type of sailing are you into: dinghy racing and/or day-sailing; family/club cruising; coastal racing; offshore (long-distance) cruising; serious blue-water racing?

3. How much can you afford? Remember there will be substantial ongoing maintenance costs as well as the capital investment. When a salesman tells you a boat is built of low-maintenance materials he is using a relative term. There is no such thing as a no-maintenance boat.

4. Where will the boat be kept when not in use? This again may incur an ongoing cost because a large or fixed-keel sailboat will need a marina berth or swing mooring. A trailer-boat will need space at home where it won't be blocking the driveway or filling the garage when you need to work on the car.

5. What sized boat will be right for your needs? This is related to questions 2, 3 and 4, but is especially important in a family boat. You don't

Above: Most popular of all small yachts is the Laser, available in six versions, best known being this 4.2-m (14-ft) single-hander adopted as the open dinghy class for the 1996 Olympics. *Photo: Roger Lean-Vercoe.*

Right: Safety is always the first consideration and lifejackets are a 'must' in small boats, even for such experienced sailors and strong swimmers as New Zealand Olympic 470-class representatives Jan Shearer and Fiona Galloway, pictured during a practice session. *Photo: Group Kiwi.*

need a lot of cockpit and/or deck area to enjoy the sunshine and sensations of sailing, but when it rains non-stop for three days, there's a nasty chop on the water, the kids are bored, someone has a headache and the bedding is starting to give off the familiar aroma of over-use in damp, confined conditions, you'll be glad of that aft cabin in which you can lock yourself for an hour or so, or take an aspirin and sleep off the headache.

Another point often overlooked by family boat-buyers is that young children who enjoy sailing with their parents often turn against boating when they start to grow up and become involved in other activities. Your chances of holding their interest and keeping the family together are definitely better if there is room aboard for them to be on their own or with friends.

If you have any doubt about the boat being big enough to meet your needs, don't buy. Better to choose one you know to be big enough even if the budget demands that it be older or less lavishly equipped.

Dinghies and small centreboarders

If the yacht is for a young person — say up to about 15 years old — you will almost certainly want a small, one-person dinghy that is safe, simple to rig, rugged and easily manhandled on and off its trailer. Perhaps an Optimist: 2.13-m (7-ft) long, popular the world over, easy to sail, forgiving in its habits, stable, but not particularly fast. In the UK there is the solid 3-m (10-ft) Mirror, the Cadet, or, if you want something light and easily carried on the car roof, the 3.4-m (11-ft 3-in.) polypropylene Topper weighing around 45-kg (100-lb).

In the US the range includes the tiny Tadpole, a wooden lapstrake six-footer (1.8m) with a simple rig for sailing and/or rowing and weighing a miniscule 20.4kg (45lb), and the fibreglass Jollyboats.

Most popular of all is the Laser, available world-wide in up to six versions from 4.2m (14ft) to 5.19m (16ft), the former suitable for one or two people, the later capable of carrying up to six. In the UK alone there are more than 1200 clubs with

Laser fleets. However, it is a performance dinghy and not suitable for rank beginners. The same applies to other Olympic and high-performance racing dinghies such as the Europe, Finn, Fireball, Flying 15, Javelin, etc.

If more than one member of the family is keen on sailing, the range of dinghies available widens dramatically. The Firefly is seen to be a good two-person sailboat in both the US and UK; the 3.8-m (12-ft 6-in.) Marlin 12 is a relatively inexpensive family sailer, as are the Blue Peter and International Cadet in the UK, or the Sunfish, Sandpiper, Barnett 1400, Jollyboat and Flying Scot in the US.

Of course, there are also the catamarans, most notable perhaps being the Hobies, in six sizes from 3.9m (13ft) to 6.4m (21ft).

There are as many types of small sailboat as there are types of small car — probably more —

Above: Sailing a dinghy is fun, but not when this happens! Most dinghy sailors find themselves in a capsize situation at some time, but there is little danger so long as you (and your crew) are wearing lifejackets, don't panic, and know the righting drill. *Photo: Roger Lean-Vercoe.*

Right: Sooner or later all dinghy sailors capsize. When it happens (A-B), don't panic. Make sure you keep hold of the boat as you swim or work your way round to the centreboard (C). Climb onto the centreboard, grab the gunwhale or sheet (D) and heave. The mainsheet must be free to run and as the boat comes upright, clamber aboard quickly before it goes over the other way. Steady yourself in the cockpit, bail out as much water as you can, haul in the mainsheet, and you're away sailing again.

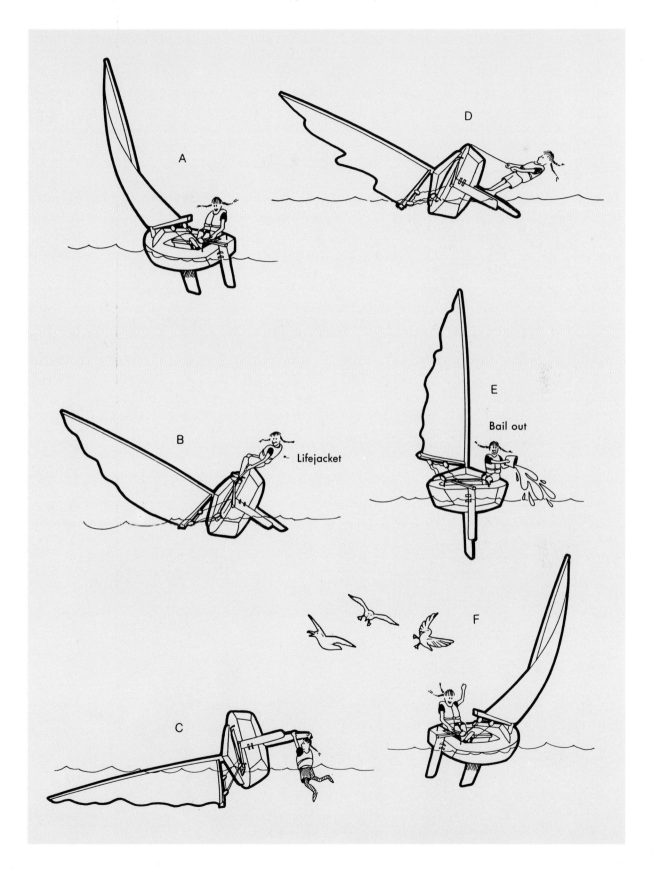

so shop around and when you see something you think suits you, ask someone who already owns one what they like and don't like about it. Best of all, take one for a test sail.

Sailing a dinghy is great fun, but safety must always be the first consideration, and the first rule is that even the strongest swimmers must wear a lifejacket at all times. Lifejackets are to a dinghy what seat-belts are to a car.

You must also know how to handle a capsize. (See page 57)

Trailer-sailers

After the dinghy and open day-sailers come the trailer-yachts, suitable for overnight or weekend cruising and racing in harbours and other sheltered waters. Trailer-yachts were very popular in the 1960s and '70s, lost a little ground in the '80s, but now seem to be making a comeback. The obvious advantages are their relatively low cost, yet with room enough for the average family; portability; no marina/mooring costs; light weight and, perhaps most importantly, versatility, i.e., the ability to perform well as a family cruiser or, with the addition of a spinnaker and a reasonably competent crew, as an exciting harbour racer. Like centreboard dinghies, they can be taken into very shallow water, or even onto the mud or beach, though raising the centreboard obviously reduces the space inside.

Virtually all the well known sailboat designers and production boatbuilders have at least one trailer-sailer in their portfolio, and the choice once again comes down to the size of your pocket, the size of your family and perhaps the size of your house and car. Silly as it sounds, there are people who have bought a trailer-sailer only to discover too late that their six-cylinder car won't shift it or their gateway/driveway won't accommodate it.

One word of warning: trailer-sailers are sheltered-water craft and in rough conditions can be dangerous in the hands of a beginner with no experience of handling centreboard sailboats.

Keelboats

Alongside the questions of cost and size, the keelboat buyer needs to put a lot of thought into what the boat is to be used for. A lightweight harbour racer will probably be totally unsuited to long-distance cruising. If you spend a lot of time sailing alone, you'll need an easily-handled boat with a fairly simple rig ... which means you'll probably miss out on the club's fully-crewed points prizes. On the other hand, a 68-footer with GPS, Satnav, pedestal winches, twin-wheel steering and a sail wardrobe which includes five spinnakers, is likely to present a few problems of overkill if all your sailing is within sight of land and from one crowded mooring to another.

There are a lot of good all-round keel yachts in the 7.6–12.2m (25–40ft) range, usually built of fibreglass or similar low-maintenance composite materials, with comfortable below-deck accommodation for five or six people, a decent galley, enclosed toilet, deep, safe cockpit and

Left: A modern cruiser/racer cockpit, with solid guard-rails, dodger for protection from wind and spray, stern boarding platform and hinged ladder for swimmers. *Photo: Group Kiwi.*

Right: Even on this big, broad-beamed cruising catamaran, all sail controls are led back through the windscreen to the top of the bridge deck so no one need be on the foredeck in rough weather. *Photo: Group Kiwi.*

simple sloop rig. Nowadays, all sail controls lead back to the cockpit so no one has to be on the foredeck in rough conditions. Such boats are sound, safe family cruisers but capable of exciting racing and with active class associations organising year-round racing and social events.

Motorsailers

Once considered to be strictly for the elderly and retired sailor, motorsailers have gained in popularity in recent times, especially with people with young families who have limited sailing experience and enjoy the security of an engine powerful enough to reach home or shelter when the weather turns nasty.

At what point a sailboat becomes a motorsailer is hard to define, but most have a covered wheelhouse and engine power (though not necessarily speed) equivalent to a launch of similar proportions. They are considerably heavier (and more expensive) than similar-sized sailboats.

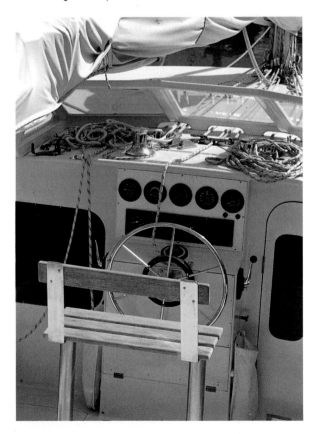

Research your requirements thoroughly

Whatever your choice, racing or cruising, dinghy, trailer-sailer, multihull or keelboat, do read as many sailing books as you can get hold of. (Most public libraries have a good selection.) Look for those that put everything in simple terms and don't bother with the highly technical works, because by the time you have swotted up on hydrodynamics, aerodynamics, match-racing tactics, design theory and construction techniques, you'll be blinded with science and probably totally confused.

For me the basics of sailing were, and still are, quite straightforward. Once you understand them, you can go on to read about and appreciate the more technical aspects, though few of these are necessary to enjoy sailing to its fullest.

No longer considered to be strictly for the elderly and retired, the motorsailer is gaining in popularity, especially with people who enjoy the feeling of security that comes from an engine powerful enough to reach shelter when the weather turns nasty. *Photo: Roger Lean-Vercoe.*

Summary

- Never settle for a boat too small to meet your needs.
- Are you sure you need a sailboat, not a powerboat?
- There is no such thing as a no-maintenance boat.
- Allow for the changing interests of your family.
- Consider the options before selecting a class of dinghy.
- Don't be blinded by science, it will only put you off sailing.

Chapter 4

BUYING
SECONDHAND

HAVING discussed in the previous chapter some of the factors involved in choosing the right type of boat for your particular sailing needs, let's now assume you are among the vast majority of people unable to enjoy the luxury of ordering their yacht custom-built or brand new and who therefore have to search for it among the 'Boats for sale' advertisements and/or the brokers' yards.

Buyer beware!

Checking ads in newspapers and magazines and browsing among the brokers' yards can be pleasant and instructive, but beware, for buying a secondhand boat, especially an older type, is fraught with potential problems, not all of which

are obvious from a routine inspection. If the slick paint job on the hull of that three-year-old fibreglass 30-footer conceals the beginnings of osmosis or, in the case of a wooden hull, the pinhole doorways of teredo worm, then you have bought trouble — capital 'T' Trouble. At best you will arrive at your mooring one good sailing Saturday morning to find only the mast and cabin above water; at worst you could be courting tragedy. I have just read, within a relatively short period of time, two reports of boats suddenly sinking while on trial in the hands of would-be buyers. Both had fatal consequences and were found to be the result of wooden hulls literally falling apart from rot.

Apart from the hull itself, the potential ailments of masts, rigging, interior furnishings and fittings, auxiliary engines, electronics, toilets (a frequent source of trouble, especially in older boats), galleys, skin fittings, propeller shafts, rudders, keel bolts, chainplates, winches, sails, fuel and water tanks, stanchions, guardrails, cabin windows and hatches, mast-steps, ground tackle and galloping electrolysis just don't bear thinking about.

Insist on a survey

The single most important step in buying a secondhand yacht is to insist on a survey, when an expert will winkle out all these problems and give you an estimate of what extra cost would be involved in putting them right. Reliable brokers and dealers welcome surveys which, contrary to popular belief, are not just sought by buyers of the biggest and most expensive craft. Most marine surveyors charge between 6 and 10 per cent of the sale price ... not expensive insurance against buying something which could fall apart on your first family outing.

It's worth noting here the difference between brokers and agents or dealers. The former rarely handle dinghies or small sailboats and they sell only 'on behalf'. In other words, brokers do not own the boats they sell, so you are unlikely to be subjected to the same sales pressure you would be from a dealer. A broker will handle all negotiations between buyers and seller, arrange the finance and survey, draw up the contract and bill of sale, collect money from the buyer and, when the deal is complete, deduct the commission and forward the balance to the seller. On the other hand, if you are trading one boat for another, you may find it difficult working through a broker because, like selling a house, you will either have to find a buyer for your existing boat or have a sympathetic bank manager before you can buy the one you want.

Dealers buy and sell in much the same way as car dealers. They are mostly involved in powerboats, but may also have an interest in small sailing dinghies and trailer-sailers. They buy their stock, so, like car dealers, they often carry out repairs, re-paints, re-fitting, etc., to make a boat more attractive to potential buyers. Take great care when buying from a dealer.

Agents represent a particular manufacturer or boatbuilder. Their job is to sell new boats but they usually have a few 'trade-ins' looking for buyers.

Whether buying privately, or through a broker or dealer, don't be taken in by any loose advertising or references to Lloyd's or ABS (American Bureau of Shipping). A survey is always needed and sales gimmicks like 'built in Lloyd's/ABS approved materials' or 'to Lloyd's/ABS standards' are meaningless. Only a

Left: Everything looks fine, but the potential ailments of masts, winches, stanchions, guardrails, hatches, ground tackle and a hundred other items of gear and equipment make the services of a reliable marine surveyor an essential pre-requisite to buying secondhand. *Photo: Group Kiwi.*

Right: Browsing among the brokers' boats can be a pleasant way to begin the search for that 'Ideal Sailboat'. *Photo: Group Kiwi.*

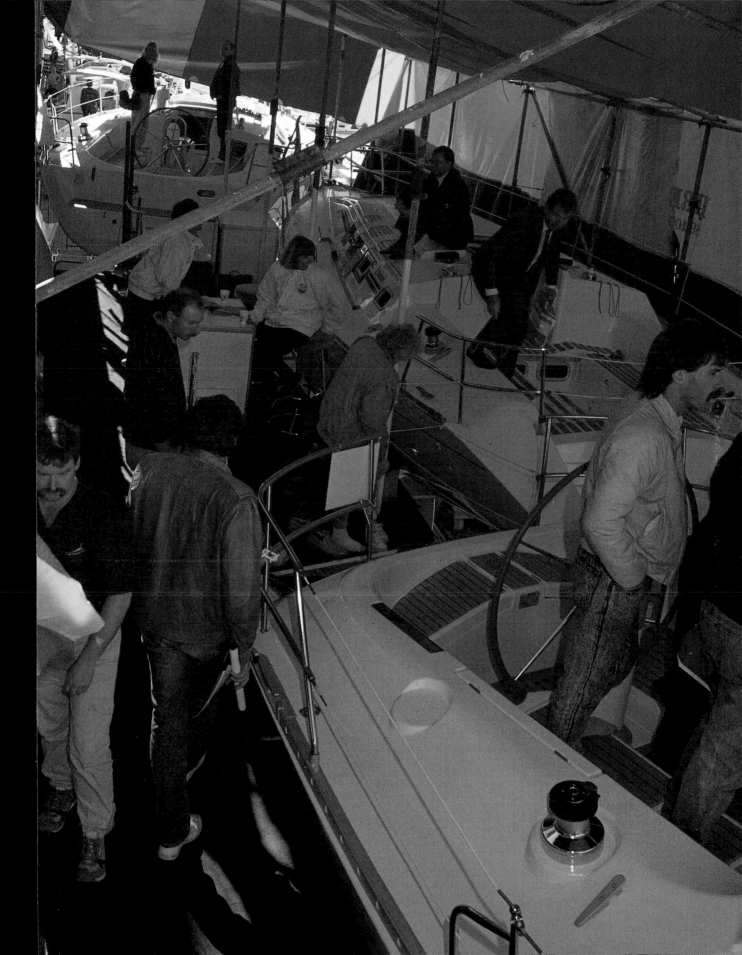

Lloyd's or ABS certificate counts and even then, once certified, a yacht must be examined two years after construction and completely re-certified two years later. So if your yacht is offered as 'Lloyd's certified', ask to see the certificate and make sure it is current. If it was issued 10 years ago and has not been renewed since, then it is worthless.

The marine surveyor's job

How will your surveyor earn his fee? First, if the boat is on a mooring or marina, it will need to be hauled out. Don't accept a surveyor's report if the boat has not been out of the water. The surveyor will use a metal spike, mallet and torch to probe around inside the hull, check the bilges, keel bolts, frames, bulkheads, skin fittings and plumbing. He'll poke behind lockers, etc., to detect any signs of rot or deterioration/damage to the hull itself. (Experienced surveyors can often detect trouble simply by smelling it.) Outside, he will make sure there is no wear in the rudder and propeller bearings, excessive play in the shaft, or

signs of electrolysis.

Back on board he will examine the chainplates to make sure they are securely attached, that they have not moved and that the eye at the top to which the rigging screw is attached is not worn thin. He will go over all deck fittings, stem-head roller, furling gear, winches, toe and hand-rails, ventilators and hatches, carefully checking the latter for leaks. If he is thorough, he will examine the mast-step for any signs of leakage through the collar, which can spread water into the deck-head and cause rot to set in undetected. Stanchions and guardrails need careful scrutiny, and if the hull and decks are glass reinforced plastics (GRP), the wooden pads to which the stanchions are secured should be examined for splits or rust 'bleed' from the bolts. The join between hull and deck should show no sign of leaks or, even worse, separation.

The surveyor will go up the mast in a bosun's chair to check all rigging, spreaders, sail tracks, sheaves, mast-head fittings, etc. Back on deck, he will pull all sails out of their bags and assess them for wear and tear. (The only real way to check

Left: If the boat is on a marina it will need to be hauled out for the hull to undergo a thorough and reliable inspection. *Photo: Group Kiwi.*

Above: A marine surveyor uses his mallet to check a GRP hull for signs of de-lamination or water penetration. *Photo: Group Kiwi.*

sails for shape, however, is to go sailing.)

The auxiliary is important. It should be clean, not leaking oil, and with all hoses, filters and other fittings (particularly the exhaust system) in good condition. The surveyor will visually check all electrics associated with the engine, as well as any generators and other major items of electrical gear, but he probably won't go into the fine detail of their condition as this requires specialised expertise and test equipment. Surveyor's reports usually include an appropriate disclaimer to this effect.

Petrol auxiliaries (other than outboards) are rare these days, but an older boat may still be fitted with one. Remember that petrol engines are more expensive to run and maintain than diesels, and the fire risk is greater. Also, diesels depend on the electrical system only for starting and battery charging.

Stand and watch the surveyor while he does his job, but don't get in his way. Like house surveyors, they prefer to do their own thing.

The sailing trial

Assuming you receive a satisfactory surveyor's report, your next step is to ask for a sailing trial. In the owner's presence, operate all — and I mean *all* — equipment: run the motor, make sure all gauges and instruments are registering and that the radio, radar and other navigational aids are fully functional. Remember, the surveyor won't have been able to test any of these things with the boat out of the water.

Switch off the engine and start sailing. Does everything feel as it should? Is the boat reasonably well balanced and not likely to tear your arms out of their sockets because of excessive weather helm? If the boat is an older design, don't be put off if the sails are not of the very latest shape and materials. Just make sure they are in a good state of repair and that they set as they should.

Back at the mooring, check every item of equipment on board against an inventory which the broker should provide. If you are not happy about the condition of, say, the lifejackets, the fire extinguishers, the dinghy or anything else, say so. If anything is missing, note it on the inventory. All these details must be sorted out to everyone's satisfaction before any money changes hands.

If the owner agrees to replace a faulty or missing item, make sure you agree on whether the replacement should be new or otherwise. Many a buyer has been caught by the phrase 'subject to replacement of anchor warp [or whatever]' only to find that the replacement is just as old and worn as the original.

Finally, if the boat is on a mooring or marina, ask the owner to allow it to stay for an agreed period after the deal is completed so that you have time to find a place of your own in which to keep it.

Who pays for what?

You, as the buyer, must of course pay the surveyor. Depending on where the boat is, you may have to pay travelling costs, so make sure that when the surveyor arrives he is met by someone who has the appropriate authority to board and, if necessary, move the boat ... and who has the right keys!

The broker's commission is paid by the seller.

Suppose the surveyor finds, say, a small patch of osmosis in the fibreglass hull. You may decide on one of the following courses of action:
1. Pull out of the deal.
2. Ask for the necessary repair to be made by the seller at no cost to you.
3. Accept the boat as is, but at a price reduced enough to cover the cost of the repair.

Any defect or missing item of equipment is subject to negotiation, but you must be aware of it before you buy and be fully aware of what it will cost to remedy at a later date. Above all, get everything in writing. Don't accept verbal assurances, no matter how genuine and honest the seller and/or broker.

Summary

• When you find the boat you like, keep in mind its further resale value. Is it a popular class and/or by a well-known designer? Has it been on the market for a long time, and if so, why?

• Insist on a satisfactory survey as part of the contract.

• If buying privately and not personally acquainted with the seller, seek proof of ownership and make sure there are no hire purchase payments or other debts outstanding on the boat. Have all documents relevant to the sale checked by a lawyer before signing or parting with any money. If dealing through a broker, make sure he has a good reputation.

• Always insist on a complete inventory and check it carefully before making any payments.

• Be prepared to bargain over any defects and/or missing gear, but make sure that any agreement reached is clearly detailed in the sale documents.

• Ask for use of the existing marina/mooring for an agreed period of time to allow you to arrange your own mooring and have the vessel moved.

Chapter 5

THE
DO-IT-YOURSELF
BUILDER

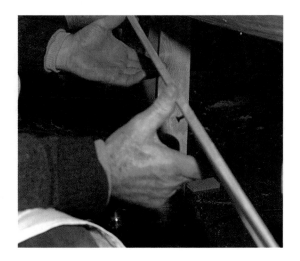

FOR MANY people, the 'Joy of Sailing' is matched only by the 'Joy of Building'.

Building your own boat is certainly a scene with which I am familiar. While still a youngster, I helped finish off my own Z-Class dinghy from a basic hull, and later I built myself two small keelers, *Bandit* and *Oliver Twist*. Even as a professional yachtsman, I have been closely involved in the design and construction of two British maxis plus three more in New Zealand, including my 1990 Whitbread Round the World Race winner, *Steinlager 2*.

Do-it-yourself boatbuilding projects begin long before actual construction work, and much

thought, planning, budgeting and careful shopping for materials is needed if you are not to finish up deeply disappointed and possibly even further in debt than if you had opted to buy a stock, ready-to-sail boat.

Early decisions

As with buying, the first decision must be the type and size of yacht you want and, perhaps more importantly, can afford to build. Here you have an advantage over the ready-to-sail buyer in that you can stretch your budget over the whole building period, be it eight or nine months or several years. As a result you can probably build bigger and equip to a higher standard than if you were buying new or secondhand. Even while building, you should be constantly on the lookout for deals and bargains that will enable you to keep costs down without compromising your original ideas on materials and equipment.

The next important decision will be hull material and here again, projected use and cost are the major factors, closely followed by your own knowledge of, and skill at, woodworking, fibreglassing, welding, etc. Using modern adhesives and systems such as stitch-and-tape, and with a set of full-size plans specifically drawn for the amateur builder, it is possible for someone with no experience and little or no skill to assemble a kitset dinghy on the living-room floor while the rest of the family are watching television. If your ambitions go no further than a dinghy or small sailing boat, don't be put off by lack of boatbuilding experience or knowledge. A set of plans, materials list and building instructions from a reputable designer will take you through the project step-by-step as easily as building a kitset model aeroplane.

However, if your boat is to be more than just a basic sailing dinghy, you will need to consider your ability to interpret a lines drawing and detailed plans as well as your skills at working with wood, fibreglass, composites, steel or alloy. Bear in mind, too, that a hull built in any material other than steel will require to be under cover at least until it is complete and with the deck in place, so where to build becomes another hurdle to overcome before construction can begin.

For harbour and inshore racing craft, steel is heavy and impractical, as is alloy for sailboats of less than about 9-m (30-ft) LOA (overall length). Both materials require considerable specialised equipment and skill at welding if a fair hull is to be produced. Not surprisingly, then, the majority of do-it-yourself projects are in wood, GRP or composite (a combination of materials). Little more than basic machine tools are necessary for these, and if you do make a mistake during construction, it is usually possible to correct it

— which is not the case with steel and alloy.

Choosing the design

Unless you have a great deal of experience and technical know-how, don't even attempt to design your own sailboat, because your dream will almost certainly turn into a nightmare. Once you have decided what size and type of boat you want, and what materials you are best able to build in, start looking around and canvassing advice and opinions on the choice of designer. There is no substitute for sailing a boat to learn how a design works in practice, and when you ask owners/ skippers why they chose a particular design, the reply is invariably that they sailed aboard a similar one and were impressed.

Most established designers have plans for the do-it-yourself builder, and for a small fee will supply a study plan and estimate of materials cost. As well as picking a design that meets your sailing needs and aspirations, you need to be sure you can build it from the designer's drawings, so check carefully on the number and type of working drawings that come with the design. Some designers offer very many sheets of fine detail that make it easy on the first-time builder; others tend to assume some experience and leave you needing to ask a lot of questions and/or make your own assumptions . . . with possibly dire consequences!

For a boat up to about 7.3m (24ft) you could expect full-size drawings and templates for the main structural elements of the hull (frames, floors, bulkheads, etc.), but for a larger vessel you may have to loft the lines onto the floor of your building space, i.e., scale the drawings up to full size . . . a process which requires patience and a certain level of skill.

Don't be afraid to send a designer a rough sketch and detailed brief of your requirements. If he can't match them exactly from his existing portfolio, he will probably suggest a modification to meet your needs without the considerable expense of commissioning a one-off design.

A word of warning: don't buy plans with the intention of making your own changes, unless

Above: The Joy of Sailing can be matched by the Joy of Building — but beware, many do-it-yourselfers wind up in debt! *Photo: Group Kiwi.*

Below: You may not match the lifetime skills of this master boatbuilder, but don't be put off by lack of experience or knowledge. It is surprising what even a beginner can achieve with a set of plans, materials list and instructions from a reputable designer *Photo: Boating World.*

you first tell the designer what those changes are. Altering the lines or layout with a consequent re-distribution of weight and points of balance can drastically upset the safety and performance of a sailboat as well as reduce its resale value. Most marinas and moorings have their well-publicised 'dogs' which testify not so much to their owners' poor do-it-yourself workmanship as to their having made their own modifications to their designers' plans.

Where to build

Whatever type and size of boat you are building, a shed in your own backyard is the ideal venue. Remember, however, that once the boat is built you have to get it out of the shed. Countless garages and sheds have been dismantled, hedges, fences and walls demolishd, trees uprooted and neighbours enraged because an enthusiastic do-it-yourself boatbuilder failed to work out how he intended getting his handiwork out of the shed and into the water.

Excellent home-boatbuilding projects can be completed under a temporary plastic shelter, but two things need to be considered before you start collecting old timber and rolls of polythene sheeting.

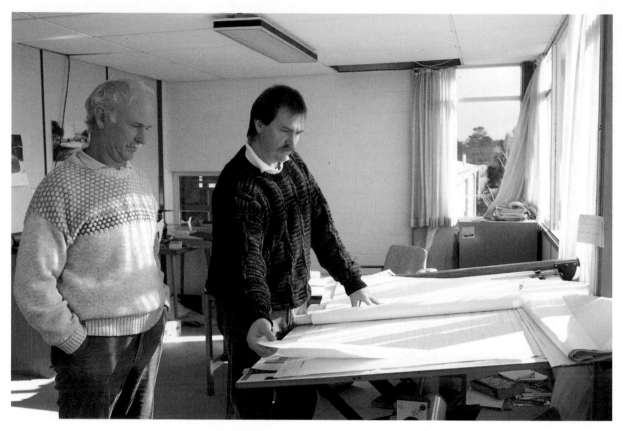

1. Such structures are invariably unsightly and, even if temporary, fatal to neighbourhood relationships, so before choosing the temporary-shelter option, seek neighbours' approval and co-operation as well as local government planning permission.

2. Know what you are doing. Not only can a storm destroy your shelter along with the half-finished boat inside it, but materials such as resins, adhesives and paints are extremely susceptible to condensation and humidity during the curing process. Many cases of osmosis (fibreglass 'boat pox') result from humidity having formed a film of water, often virtually invisible, between the laminations during construction.

A final word about the building shed. If the boat is to be 9.1-m (30-ft) LOA × 2.4-m (8-ft) beam, then a 9.7-m (32-ft) × 2.7-m (9-ft) shed is useless. You must have room for a decent-sized workbench and to be able to manoeuvre lengths of timber, etc., into place. You also need to be able to operate power sanders, paintbrushes,

rollers, etc., comfortably and safely while working on the outside of the hull.

Check that you have safe and adequate lighting and power. Ask a qualified electrician to install and/or check temporary cables, power-points and other fixed installations, which should comply with local authority regulations. When using power tools, they should be connected to a transformer or residual current interrupter.

Tools

Most boatbuilding does not require expensive or highly specialised tools, but always buy the best you can afford. A basic toolkit might include hammers and mallets, handsaws, hacksaws, planes, chisels, screwdrivers, brace and bit, hand-drill, spokeshave, a selection of rasps and files, adjustable and fixed-jaw pliers, bullnose plane, square, dividers, spirit-level, Surforms and G-clamps (lots of them in a range of sizes). Power tools make the job easier: electric drill (with holesaw attachments), router (to radius edges), bandsaw (preferably with 12-mm skip-tooth blade), belt and/or orbital sander, small circular saw and a grinder. You'll also need a good supply of pencils, including the carpenter's type.

Use the grinder to keep saws, chisels, drill bits, knives, etc., sharp, and make sure that spirit-levels, rulers and other measuring devices are clean, undamaged, and never used for anything other than the purpose for which they were intended.

Your working area should be kept uncluttered and swept free of sawdust, shavings, offcuts, bits of wire, loose screws, etc., at the end of each working session.

Wear shatter-proof goggles, gloves, fume and dust masks, and other personal protective equipment whenever power tools and certain materials and processes are in use (e.g., resins, adhesives, solvents, paint). Of course you will need a good supply of paintbrushes, buckets and cleaning materials, rollers, solvents, etc. I also strongly recommend having a good quality fire-extinguisher within easy reach at all times.

Left: Don't be afraid to let your designer and builder know exactly what you want. Top boatbuilders like New Zealanders Terry and Mick Cookson, responsible for many of the world's most successful America's Cup, Admirals Cup and Whitbread ocean racers, spend much of their time discussing clients' ideas and requirements, poring over sketches, plans and specifications before building actually begins. *Photo: Group Kiwi.*

Below: Unless they are of the cordless type, power tools should always be connected to the mains supply through a transformer or residual current interruptor, even if nowhere near the water. *Photo: Group Kiwi.*

Kitsets

A misnomer is that they are not kitset in the accepted modellers' use of the word but a useful 'half-way' method of building a boat for the handyman who feels that a hull is beyond his abilities and/or who wants to reduce building time. A fibreglass kitset can be a bare hull, hull and keel, or virtually any stage of construction up to the finished boat. There are cost advantages (though they decrease significantly depending on how much is included in the 'kit') and joining a class owners' association usually allows you to take advantage of bulk-buying agreements.

With a kitset you can usually make minor alterations to the interior layout without seriously affecting the balance or performance of the boat and you can be on the water enjoying your sailing even before you have the time and/or money to complete the accommodation in terms of bunks, galley furnishings, shelves, lockers, etc.

Costs and budget

Whatever construction method and hull material you decide on, the hull and deck will represent probably less than a third of the cost of the sailaway boat. The real bills will come with the interior plumbing, engineering and electrical installations, deck gear, rig, sails, engine and navigational instruments. There is virtually no limit to what can go onto or into your sailboat to make life safer and more comfortable, but the following list is a starting-point for budget calculations.

A guide to essentials

Spars: mast, boom, spinnaker poles, jockey poles, headsail foil system.

Sails: mainsail, headsails, storm jib, trysail, spinnakers, sailbags, battens, sail covers, ties.

Standing rigging: shrouds, forestay, backstay, rigging screws, toggles, seizing wire, shackles.

Running rigging: halyards, sheets, general cordage, clips and shackles.

Hydraulics: backstay, vang, etc., pumps, gauges and piping.

Winches: halyard and sheet winches, mounting brackets, handles, handle-holders.

Deck gear: chainplates, stem-head and backstay fittings, blocks, sheet tracks, shackles, pulpit, pushpit, stanchions, hatches, steering system (tiller or wheel), ventilators, navigation lights, mooring bollard, cleats and jammers, fairleads (including roller type for anchor), fenders, two anchors (minimum), chain, anchor, warps, boat hooks, buckets, scrubbing brushes, cockpit/hatch dodgers, handrails, anchor winch, hatch washboards and lock, emergency tiller (if wheel steering fitted), steering compass (swung after launching).

General: engine and installation materials (exhaust, silencer, piping, filters, etc.), fuel tanks with shut-off valves, propeller with shaft and couplings, battery-charging alternator (fitted to engine), cockpit controls and gauges, spare fuel containers (marked), funnels and filters (marked), deck filler caps for fuel and water (marked), zinc anode for corrosion protection, plumbing for exhausts, toilet and sink outlets, fresh, saltwater and cock-pit drains, batteries and switches, electric panel, spare water containers (marked), water-tank shut-off valve, seacocks for all through-hull fittings, complete set of tools, lubricants.

Safety equipment: bilge pumps and hoses, fire blanket, fire extinguishers, flashlights, foghorn, radar reflector, lifebuoys and danbuoy, lifejackets and whistles, safety harnesses and whistles, liferaft (for blue-water sailing), distress flares, heaving lines, emergency radio beacon (EPIRB), first-aid kit.

Navigation: compasses (hand-bearing and steering), binoculars, charts, dividers, parallel rules, barometer, clock, sextant and tables, echo-sounder (or leadline), electronic sailing instruments, VHF radio and aerial, SSB radio and aerial, general-purpose receiver. For long-distance cruising: radar, satellite navigator and weather facsimile.

Galley: gimballed stove, gas controls (valves, cocks, hoses, etc.), gas bottles, sink unit and

pumps, cooking utensils, cutlery and crockery, storage containers, racks, possibly a deep-freeze and/or refrigerator. The galley should also have its own first-aid kit and fire extinguisher.

Head: marine toilet, washbasin and pumps, mirror, toilet-roll and toothbrush holders, towel rail.

Personal: sufficient bunks and storage lockers, bedding (sleeping bags preferred), pillows, squabs and lee cloths for bunks, floor coverings, wet-weather clothing and plenty of towels, non-skid deck shoes and/or sea-boots, fishing gear.

Finally, don't forget the *dinghy* (inflatable or rigid) with oars, a good *bosun's chair* along with *other maintenance items* such as paints, glues, sealants, engine spares (plugs, hose, hose-clamps, etc.), a variety of sizes and types of fastenings, and a sail-repair kit.

The hull and deck represent less than a third of the cost of your boat. The real bills come when you start adding the deck gear! *Photo: Group Kiwi.*

Summary

• Take time to research the type and size of yacht you want.

• Choose a hull material you know you can work with.

• Seek advice and opinions before choosing a design or designer.

• Never change building plans without consulting the designer.

• Have a suitable building site and the right tools.

• Budget for the greater part of your expense to go into deck gear, plumbing, engineering and electrical systems.

Chapter 6

THE CRUISING YACHT

MOST sailors rarely 'compete' in their sport. For them, and even for many of us who gain our measure of fame from taking part in the America's Cup, Whitbread, Olympics or other high-profile racing events, the real joy of sailing is cruising. Let's face it, a racing yacht can be all bumps, hollows and other distortions — wet, uncomfortable and beyond the control of anyone other than an experienced helmsman and crew — but a well-designed cruiser is invariably delightful to look at and to sail. Unlike a racing boat, it won't be a temperamental lightweight product of complex rating rules, but will be safe, seaworthy, comfortable, relatively easy to handle and able to carry a reasonable load of home comforts without too much effect on its performance.

The hull design

The lines (shape) of a cruising hull should look clean and preferably with an elongated keel rather than the narrow fin-type, making it easier to lean against a sea-wall or post and scrub the bottom clear of marine growth while the tide is out.

Moderate draft is another attribute of good cruising design. A 10-m cruising boat will create problems if it needs more than 1.8m of water in which to float. In the Bahamas, for instance, a draft of more than 2m precludes sailing over much of the Bahama Bank, a huge area of idyllic, island-

A classic contrast in style and function: the cruiser *(nearest camera)*, with its elongated keel, slack bilges and deep forefoot, has many advantages over its racing counterpart alongside, even though the latter's flat hull sections and fin keel will make it a better windward performer. *Photo: Group Kiwi.*

studded water. While shallow or moderate draft may not be quite as good to windward as its deep-draft, fin-keel racing counterpart, this disadvantage is far outweighed by other advantages. The well-designed cruiser should also be stable and reasonably stiff, i.e., not prone to heel (lean over) at the first puff of wind and hence require constant reefing and/or sail changes.

Popular materials and construction methods

All common hull materials and methods of construction can be used, and there is a considerably higher proportion of steel and wooden craft among cruisers than in a racing fleet.

Steel

Steel has long been a popular choice for blue-water (long-distance) cruising craft 9.14m (30ft) or bigger, mainly because its tremendous strength enables it to take the occasional brush with a wharf or harbour wall without sustaining too much damage. It is also the least expensive material in which to build. On the downside is the fact that steel corrodes in a marine atmosphere and it is therefore essential to maintain a good paint finish, touching up scrapes or gouges as soon as they occur. There are also design limitations; rounded sections ('wineglass' shapes) are possible but their compound curves require specialised and expensive equipment to achieve. As a result, most steel hulls are of hard chine construction, i.e., shapes developed from flat plate welded at the seam, or chine.

The weight of a steel hull relative to its equivalent in other materials is a subject of much debate. While a piece of steel is heavier than the same-sized piece of wood, aluminium or fibreglass,

Left: Moderate draft is an attribute of good cruising design, especially if the vessel is to be used in the shallow waters of many of the world's most popular cruising grounds, such as these around Antigua in the Lesser Antilles. *Photo: Roger Lean-Vercoe.*

Below: A well-designed cruiser will be safe, seaworthy and comfortable in all but the worst conditions. *Photo: Roger Lean-Vercoe.*

on a strength-to-weight ratio, i.e., the weight of a given structural member needed to achieve the required strength, steel can come out ahead.

Steel tends to transmit higher levels of water and marine life sounds than other materials and steel cruisers therefore often have a reputation for being noisy below deck. Some critics also argue that they are prone to 'sweating' (excessive condensation) in cold weather, although both these problems are due more to inadequate insulation and ventilation than to the steel itself.

Wood

Every port and mooring has its fleet of wooden-hulled cruising boats, many built by their owners, lovingly crafted in the most versatile and forgiving of all boatbuilding materials. Sadly, as the world accepts the need to conserve native forests, good boatbuilding timbers are becoming scarce and hence expensive. For the true sailor there will never be anything quite like the smell, feel and sense of security that comes with a heavyweight cruising hull built from traditional lapstrake/

Left: Two aspects of the downside of steel construction — a constant battle against saltwater corrosion, plus the design difficulty of achieving rounded or 'wineglass' sections. Most steel hulls are, like this one, of welded flat plate, or hard-chine, construction. *Photo: Group Kiwi.*

Right: Wooden hulls need good initial protection and more regular maintenance than fibreglass, steel or aluminium, but modern marine paints and the practice of sheathing wooden hulls with epoxy resins and fibreglass have greatly increased their durability while maintaining all the practical and aesthetic qualities of the material. *Photo: Group Kiwi/Boating World.*

Below left: The majority of modern, low-cost, high-quality production sailboats, like these from the giant French Jeanneau organisation, pop from their moulds as complete glass-reinforced plastic shells, often including major accommodation elements as well. *Photo: Group Kiwi.*

Below right: Popular for large ocean racers and cruisers, aluminium is expensive but has the strength of steel for about half its weight. *Photo: Group Kiwi.*

clinker (overlapping) or carvel (edge-to-edge) planks over solid frames and bulkheads.

By its very nature, wood needs good initial protection and more regular care and attention than fibreglass, aluminium or even steel, but modern paint technology, along with the now-common practice of sheathing wooden hulls with epoxy resin and fibreglass, greatly increases the length of time a hull can be in the water between repaints.

Aluminium

Aluminium is expensive but offers most of the strength and durability attributes of steel, with the additional bonus of light weight. An aluminium hull weighs about half that of its size/strength equivalent in steel. Still popular for large, maxi-type racing craft, an aluminium hull has greater load-carrying capacity than either wood or steel, while a high degree of stability can be achieved because of its low centre of gravity. It requires little or no painting and maintenance

other than below-waterline anti-fouling.

Its main disadvantage is cost. Aluminium is not normally produced in the profile shapes needed for boatbuilding and often has to be custom-milled and/or extruded for a particular project. Consequently it is the most expensive of all hull materials, other than the latest specialised carbon-fibre laminates.

Apart from cost, a disadvantage for cruising is that around the world only a limited number of boatyards are capable of repairing aluminium hulls — indeed, about 80 per cent of countries have no facilities at all for handling them. Aluminium is an excellent heat conductor and its low melting point means that, unlike steel, the fire risk is at least as great as for wood or fibreglass.

Fibreglass

Not surprisingly, in these days of low-cost, high-quantity production, the majority of sailboats, including cruisers, are of fibreglass (GRP) construction, popped from a mould in the form of a complete shell, either solid, laminated, or a

Above left: An efficient roller-reefing headsail system makes sail-handling easier, especially on vessels up to about 10m (33ft). *Photo: Group Kiwi.*

Above right: New Zealand sailmaker Chris Lee at work. Note bobbins of dark-coloured thread contrasting with the yellow sailcloth, a way of identifying areas of chafe early enough for effective repairs to be made. *Photo: Group Kiwi.*

Right: Sails are a complex and often controversial subject, but each year thousands of young people learn how to handle sails and something of the importance of their design, shape, and construction, by going to sea aboard traditional square-rigged training vessels such as Britain's *Winston Churchill*, Chile's famous *Esmerelda*, or *(pictured here)*, the New Zealand 33-m (108-ft) steel topsail schooner *Spirit of Adventure*, in which more than 12,000 youngsters have so far learned the basics of sails and sailing. *Photo: The Spirit of Adventure Trust.*

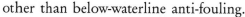

'sandwich' filled with plastic foam. GRP is the basis of virtually all 'kitset' hulls and offers many advantages for the cruising sailboat, not least being resistance to rot and teredo worm, the ease with which scrapes and minor damage can be repaired, and the fact that, unlike other materials, the hull is a complete shell without joins or seams other than at the hull/keel and hull/deck.

Like all other materials, GRP does require maintenance by way of regular scraping, sanding and anti-fouling, and it must be moulded in a temperature and humidity-controlled environment to eliminate the risk of osmosis or, even worse, de-lamination. As mentioned in a previous chapter, before buying a GRP-hulled boat you should always seek a surveyor's report. Unlike wood, steel or aluminium, poor-quality GRP moulding is not easily detected.

Rig

A cruising rig must first and foremost be easily handled. For an overall length of 10m (33ft) or less, the single-masted sloop (one headsail) or cutter (two or more headsails) is the simplest, cheapest and easiest for a small crew to handle, particularly when fitted with a reliable roller-reefing headsail system. Over 10m a sloop or cutter may still be best, although I favour the ketch (two masts). It is slightly more expensive but extremely versatile and the sails, being small, are easily handled.

Some purists like gaff rigs with traditional fittings, but for ease of operation and maintenance, stick to modern ideas and materials — at least until you have been sailing for a few years and have formed your own ideas as to what suits you best.

Roller-reefing/furling headsails offer two major advantages for the cruising yacht:

1. Only two headsails are needed instead of four or five.

2. Sail can be reduced without anyone leaving the cockpit.

Roller-furling mainsails that roll inside the special mast extrusion are gaining popularity among cruising sailboat owners, but they are expensive and I have yet to be convinced that they are necessary on anything but the largest craft.

Standing rigging should be 1 x 19 galvanised, or preferably stainless steel, wire — not rod. For halyards, I recommend 6 x 19 galvanised wire, which is less likely to produce sharp snags and gives ample warning of a break. Stainless usually goes with a bang. The only maintenance needed for galvanised-wire halyards is a six-monthly rub with Fisherlene or its equivalent.

For a roller-reefing headsail in which the halyard is part of the foil, stainless steel is essential. A damp sail rolling round galvanised wire quickly collects rust stains.

Don't try to make do with all-rope halyards on anything other than topping lifts or spinnakers. With the exception of Kevlar, all-rope halyards stretch and allow the sail to become baggy as the wind increases — the opposite of what should happen. Better to have wire spliced to a rope tail; lack of stretch in the wire, even if not winched particularly tight, produces a better-setting sail.

Sails

This is a complex and often controversial subject which depends heavily on personal preference, especially on a cruising sailboat. But briefly . . .

Sails are the driving force of any sailboat and if of initially poor design, they soon become baggy and/or misshapen and the performance of the boat suffers accordingly. Apart from shape, the construction of cruising sails is important. If you plan an overseas cruise, make sure all your sails are triple-stitched, i.e., a minimum three rows of stitching, four for larger vessels. The thread should be dark, contrasting with the sail itself. This helps identify areas of chafe at an early stage so that repairs can be made before major problems arise. Mark with a pen or pencil any areas of sail

Left: Sailbags should be oversize to cope with sails which may fit snugly when dry, but are a different proposition when wet and crumpled and you're trying to bag them in the middle of the night! These are just some of the ample bags which crowded the below-deck space aboard *Steinlager 2* during her Round the World Race-winning voyage. *Photo: Group Kiwi.*

Below: The cruising galley needs ease of access and should be a safe workplace in a seaway. Note how this well laid-out galley aboard the 15.2-m (50-ft) Bruce Farr-designed cruiser/racer *Foreign Exchange* fits snugly around its occupant who, while having room to work, has everything he needs within little more than arm's-length reach. *Photo: Group Kiwi.*

showing signs of chafe, take them to a sailmaker and ask him to add chafe patches in those areas, e.g., where the headsail rubs against the pulpit or stanchion; where the mainsail presses against the spreaders when running, or catches the spreader tips when tacking.

All fore-and-aft sails, mains, mizzens and headsails should have easily-adjusted leech cords to prevent the back end of the sail shuddering in a breeze or when reefed. Insist on a leech and foot cord in the tri-sail and storm jib; don't take 'no' for an answer. There is nothing worse than being hove-to in a blow and not being able to stop the incredible shuddering set up by incorrect leech or foot tension in either of the two sails.

Don't buy lightweight working (everyday) sails. Any extra weight in a heavier fabric or construction is worth accepting. Keep well away from sailmakers who stress the lightness of their sails. Light sails may be easy to handle but their reliability will be in doubt. Their shape may be OK first time out, but after being reefed a few times and flogged in a squall while trying to reef,

Below: The saloon table can be permanent, as aboard *Foreign Exchange*, or removable. Comfortable seats with backs are a must, and don't skimp on locker and shelf space — no boat ever has enough. Note built-in drawers in the gateleaf table, ensuring that even the small amount of space between the legs is not wasted. *Photo: Group Kiwi.*

Right: A wet-weather-gear locker, and a place for seaboots somewhere near the main hatch, are worth organising — and you'll be glad of a well-ventilated hanging locker for shore clothes. Even aboard *Steinlager 2*, where space and weight-saving were vital, each crew member had a labelled zip-bag in which to store shore clothes. *Photo: Group Kiwi.*

they'll probably look about as good as potato sacks. On any cruising sailboat reliability is of the utmost importance and a little extra weight aloft will hardly be noticed — unless you suddenly decide to enter the Admirals Cup!

Sailbags should be way oversize. Sails that fit snugly into their bags when they arrive from the loft will be a different proposition altogether when crumpled and wet and you are trying to bag them in the middle of the night.

Interior

A cruising boat must have adequate space for the number of crew it is to carry. Even if single-handing, allow for a couple of extra bunks in case you have friends to stay.

The galley should be well-ventilated, easily accessible and safe and easy to work at in a seaway. It should have adequate stowage for all necessary utensils and everyday foods, sauces, etc.

The sink(s) should drain while the boat is at a normal angle of heel or have a pumped outlet

if below the waterline when heeled. Saltwater as well as freshwater supply is essential, particularly on long-distance passages.

Bunks should be a minimum of 1.9-m (6-ft 4-in.) long and 61-cm (24-in.) wide in the middle, tapering towards the ends if necessary. They must be useable at sea, with lee cloths or boards to prevent the occupants being thrown out. It should also be possible to prop yourself up in a bunk and be able to read a book or drink a cup of coffee in comfort. Beware of cruising yachts advertised as, say, 10m LOA with '10 comfortable berths'. They might be comfortable for contortionists, but normal human beings would be well advised to try them for size before contemplating a purchase.

The toilet, or head, should be a separate compartment with its own ventilator and preferably an extractor fan. It is amazing how much total crew time is spent in the loo, so it should be of reasonable size with mirror, washbasin and seawater pump.

The saloon is generally where the crew's kit is stowed and there should be enough locker space for two sailing kitbags per person. These lockers must be easy to get at and have positive catches so they don't fly open the first time the boat heels. The saloon table can be permanent or removable, and comfortable seats with backs are a must. Adequate ventilation is important, reducing stuffiness, condensation and the chances of seasickness.

A navigation table is nice, but if no space is available the saloon table can be used. Alternatively, have a suitably-sized piece of wood stowed under a bunk and able to be placed on your knees. This works well, although obviously a purpose-built navigation area is the ideal. Stowage space for charts and navigational publications handy to where you will be navigating will make life easier, and try to find a home near the main hatch for the sextant, binoculars and hand-bearing compass.

If building your own boat or having one built for you, don't skimp on locker and shelf space. No boat ever has enough! On the subject of lockers, a wet-weather-gear locker and a place for seaboots somewhere near the main hatch is worth organising and you'll be glad of a well-ventilated hanging locker in which to keep shore clothes. Also needed are lockers for tools, screws, nails, fishing gear, torches, and all the other paraphernalia that collects aboard any cruising boat, along with a deck or cockpit locker for sails, warps, anchors and chain, chandlery, deck mop, buckets, scrubbing brushes, fuel funnels, spare water containers, boathook, engine rags, bosun's chair, etc.

Special stowage is needed for emergency equipment that may be needed in a hurry: lifejackets, safety harnesses, emergency bleeper, flares, radar reflector, medical kit, etc. Make sure this locker is clearly identified and that everyone aboard knows its location.

If the galley has a gas-stove, the gas bottles must be in their own sealed locker draining overboard. The installation must be properly carried out, with the pressure-reducing valve mounted directly on top of the bottle. Remote-controlled gas-proof electric on-off valve sets are available with a switch and indicator light mounted in the galley and valve on the bottle. When cooking is finished it is a simple matter to turn off the gas by flicking a switch. This keeps the installation safe at all times.

Extra fuel for the engine needs to be in an outside locker which drains overboard, and an outboard, if carried, needs a home, although if space is short it can be lashed to the pushpit with a waterproof cover to keep the powerhead dry.

Bilge pumps, one above and one below deck, must be readily accessible, kept clean and easy to operate. If you get backache after the first few strokes, the positioning is wrong and the pump(s) will not be of much use in an emergency. Make sure there is a sump or at least a collection point for bilge water. No sailboat remains completely dry and water from the stern gland, wet weather gear, etc., should have somewhere to go and not just slosh around the interior.

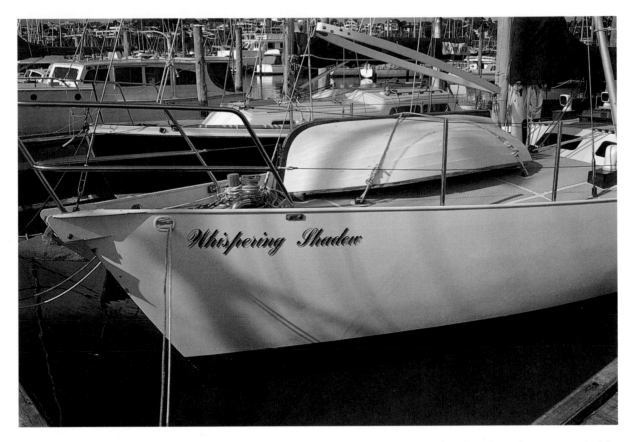

Left: Don't forget the cockpit bags for winch handles and other loose items of equipment that need to remain handy but without the risk of sliding underfoot or overboard. *Photo: Group Kiwi.*

Above: The dinghy, if of the rigid type, will normally stow upside-down (and securely lashed) on deck. *Photo: Group Kiwi.*

Don't forget the dinghy. If rigid, it can probably by stowed upside-down on deck, with lashings holding it in place. For ocean work, an inflatable is better. It can also be kept on deck, but will have a longer life stowed in a dry locker.

The engine

Finally, the engine — preferably a good diesel, marinised and correctly installed. A hard-to-get-at engine tends not to be serviced regularly, and changing worn or broken alternator belts becomes several hours of grease-stained, temper-fraying work instead of an easy 10-minute exercise.

The engine should have forward and reverse gears. Unless the boat is large, a two-bladed folding, feathering or fixed propeller will be adequate and won't detract from the vessel's sailing performance to any great degree. Batteries need their own acid-proof compartment and, like all heavy equipment on board, must stay in place in a severe knockdown or even a complete 360-degree roll. A simple fibreglass-lined plywood box will usually suffice. Engine sound-proofing is another must: listening to the whine of a diesel for hours on end adds little to the enjoyment of a cruise.

Deck equipment

Deck layout should be as simple as possible, with as many control lines, sheets and halyards coming back to the security of the cockpit as can be arranged. The cockpit itself should be comfortable and offer good protection from the weather by the use of either dodgers or lowered seating. Good visibility is important when sitting at the helm so the cabin-top should not be so high that it is impossible to see over it.

If you have a choice, go for winches one size larger than you think necessary and slightly heavier blocks, tracks and fittings than you would

Above left: Especially aboard cruising sailboats, as many control lines, sheets and halyards as possible should be led back to the security of the cockpit. *Photo: Group Kiwi.*

Left: Colour-coding can save a lot of confusion. Even aboard this Farr MRX match-racer designed for an experienced crew, all lines are colour-coded and labelled for quick identification. *Photo: Group Kiwi.*

Above: Radar, Weatherfax, Satnav, GPS — on-board electronics and navigational equipment have been influenced by computers to the point where there is virtually no limit to what can be fitted to a boat. *Photo: Group Kiwi.*

Summary

• Be familiar with the attributes of a good cruising design.
• Compare the advantages and disadvantages of various hull materials.
• Choose an easily-handled rig.
• Interior space is important . . . ample stowage, locker space, etc.
• Keep deck layout and equipment as simple as possible.
• Buy as much good-quality electronic navigation and radio equipment as you can afford.

normally require. If the budget is stretched at the time of rigging, use galvanised instead of stainless-steel shackles; they last for years if given an occasional dab of anhydrous lanolin on the threads.

When sizing cordage for sheets, anchor warps, halyards, etc., again think more of ease of handling than of breaking strains. Many sailboats have sheets that maybe won't break but are difficult to hold and pull in with wet, cold hands.

Colour-coded lines can save a lot of confusion.

Electronics

Navigation and on-board electronics have been influenced by computer technology to the point where there is virtually no limit to the sophistication and range of gear that can be fitted to a boat. Radar, Weatherfax, Satnav and even GPS (Global Positioning Satellite) are now part of even quite modest sailing craft and only your particular needs (and pocket) can dictate how much you have aboard. As an absolute minimum, however, a speedometer, log and depth-sounder are the basic electronic aids to navigation, although even these need not be electronic: good mechanical speedometer and log sets are available and a leadline will suffice as a depth-sounder.

For inshore cruising, a portable transistor radio with marine-band SS (Single Sideband) frequencies capable of receiving marine weather forecasts is all you need. A VHF (Very High Frequency) radio and/or cellphone allowing you to talk to friends or place emergency calls is nice to have but not essential. Offshore, an SSB radio with international frequencies, plus RDF (Radio Direction-Finder) are essential.

Don't forget that the more electronic equipment you carry, the more electricity you will need, and it has to come from somewhere — deck-mounted solar cells, a wind or water generator, an alternator on the engine, even, if you want the lot, additional batteries and a separate generator.

To sum up: stick to essentials, at least to start your cruising life, but buy the best you can afford and have them fitted and explained by someone with expert knowledge.

Chapter 7

GETTING READY
TO RACE

PERHAPS I have been spoilt in my sailing career. As well as my first dinghies, the family's cruisers and the keelers I built for myself, I have sailed and/or been involved in the design, construction and management of harbour racers, One Tonners, Admirals Cuppers, Whitbread maxis and the new America's Cup class. Now, having spent many years on big blue-water keelers, I would find it difficult to go back to any other kind of sailboat racing.

Ocean racing is not for everyone, however, and I would not recommend it to anyone who lacks experience of harbour and coastal competition. A good round-the-buoys sailor will usually be a

good hand in ocean racing events once he gets the distances in perspective.

Know the rules
As well as the basic experience of handling a keelboat, aspiring ocean-racing skippers and crew also need to know the racing rules, especially those relating to the start. In any ocean race a good start is of paramount importance and unless everyone aboard knows the rules, the boat stands a good chance of being disqualified or heavily penalised before the real action begins. More about the start in Chapter 8.

A few other 'rules' are necessary for anyone

Good crews are always alert, with no one catching up on lost sleep while the race is still on! *Photo: Nathan Bilow.*

looking to enjoy sailboat racing, whether on the occasional weekend aboard a round-the-buoys racer or as a longer-term member of an ocean-racing team:

• Always be punctual. If the skipper wants you aboard by 0900, don't turn up at 0915 saying you overslept or had a hard night out.
• Be alert. Don't arrive straight from an all-night party and expect to catch up on your sleep during the race.
• Be considerate. Don't expect the skipper to provide lunch if it's a day race. Offer to make the sandwiches yourself beforehand — enough for the whole crew.
• Be willing. Don't jump off and head for the nearest bar the moment mooring lines are secured. Get stuck in and help tidy up the boat. Pack sails, pump out the bilge, clean the galley thoroughly, hose down the wet-weather gear, running rigging and topsides.
• Above all, be keen. You don't have to be a 'heavy' or a deck gorilla. Simply being keen will

Above: As well as basic experience in handling a keelboat, a racing crew also needs to know the rules. *Photo: Boating World.*

Right: Keelboat racing is a team sport. Anyone who doesn't fit in should look for a place on another boat. *Photo: Franco Pace (Agence DPPI).*

usually make up for lack of physical strength and/or weight.

Keelboat racing is a team sport. Work at becoming a member of your team and if for any reason you are not fitting in, not getting on with the skipper and/or other crew, look for a place on another boat, otherwise you'll spoil it for everyone else as well as for yourself.

Let's look now at some other aspects of preparation for keelboat racing.

Boat preparation

Most keelers (there are a few exceptions) are fastest if kept light, so before a race or race series, the crew should have a thorough clean-out, keeping on board only those items necessary for racing and/or required by the rules. The barbecue and bags of charcoal may not weigh much but are better left in the club locker, along with the 25 cans of corned beef and year's supply of toilet rolls, not to mention the outboard motor, fuel for same, pots of paint, fishing gear, etc. They can be put back when the boat goes cruising.

If the diesel and water tanks are full, then, depending on the type of yacht, it may pay to pump some out (subject to rule requirements relating to pre-race time limits for pumping out water or fuel). Fuel can be stored in containers and replaced later.

The bottom of the boat must be clean and smooth. This is most important and all crew members should pitch in and spend some time on this area of preparation. The best anti-foulings are the hard types which can be scrubbed and sanded with wet and dry without coming off.

Each crew member should have an area of responsibility for checking on-board equipment before every race, i.e., sails, motor, rigging, spars, deck gear, cordage, electronics, etc.

There should be charts on board to cover the race course and they should be of the largest possible scale. The skipper should go over them with the navigator; both should know the times of high and low tide and be familiar with the latest marine weather forecast.

One crew member should be responsible for a last-minute check that the boat is carrying all necessary safety gear as required by the rules.

Sails and gear

If you own and skipper a one-design racer you may be restricted as to the number and type of sails allowed on board; different restrictions apply when racing offshore.

Left: Differing colours indicate a mix of materials strengthening stress areas of the mainsail aboard French round-the-world racer *Esprit de Liberté*, skippered by Patrick Tabarly. *Photo: Group Kiwi.*

Above: No matter what the size of yacht, its sails are its engine and you can't win races unless they are of top quality materials and construction. *Photo: Roger Lean-Vercoe.*

After the yacht itself, sails are probably the most expensive item of racing equipment. If you are a boat owner, the number and type you buy will depend on how often you race and what you can afford. Remember, however, that the sails are your 'engine' and if they are of poor quality, your chances of winning are drastically reduced.

Much the same advice on buying sails applies as for cruising sails mentioned in the previous chapter, i.e., don't always go to the sailmaker offering the cheapest quote or even to the 'big name' international lofts. Many excellent small sail lofts are operated by sailmakers who own and race a particular type of yacht and their on-going involvement and hence interest is likely to be your guarantee of service.

With massive media attention on high-profile events such as the America's Cup and Whitbread Round the World Race, much is spoken and written about so-called 'exotic' sail materials, e.g., Mylar and Kevlar. Mylar is a plastic film usually bonded to Dacron cloth during production to give the woven Dacron greater stability in all directions. Mylar sails are lighter than Dacron for the same wind strengths, they stretch little and hold their shape over a wide wind range. However, they are more expensive than Dacron and more difficult to handle. They don't like being walked on or stuffed willy-nilly into an ordinary sailbag but need to be neatly flaked into a sausage-bag. And when a Mylar sail blows out, it goes with little or no warning. For serious racing, however, the advantages of Mylar greatly outweigh the disadvantages.

Kevlar is Dupont's trade name for a manmade fibre woven into cloth in much the same way as Dacron. It has a distinctive light-brown colour and is usually glued to Mylar film in the same way as Dacron. It won't stretch and, weight for weight, is five times as strong as steel, so that a Kevlar sail can be extremely lightweight while covering a wider wind range than its Dacron equivalent. The drawbacks are:
1. Cost (about three times that of Dacron).
2. It does not like sunlight and eventually breaks down.

3. It does not like being flapped or flogged and may split if badly treated.

Despite the above, the advantages of Kevlar sails on a medium-to-large racing yacht are so great that without them you are unlikely to be competitive in a major event. Some national and other racing authorities restrict the use of Kevlar sails in an attempt to hold costs for owners, so before deciding to buy Kevlar sails make sure you are aware of your situation in this respect.

Kevlar is also used extensively by rope manufacturers, and Kevlar-cored rope is light and strong. However, it should be treated with caution as it tends to break when knotted. It is great for light spinnaker sheets on large boats but should never be used in a situation where someone could be hurt if it breaks.

Instruments

Once again my advice is simple: buy the best (rather than the most) you can afford. Nothing is more frustrating for a racing skipper than

Left: Kevlar, a manmade sail material five times as strong as steel, and identifiable by its distinctive light-brown colour, is clearly visible as reinforcement for highly-stressed areas of sail aboard the 18.3-m (60-ft) David Alan-Williams-designed trimaran, *Steinlager 1*, in this photograph taken during the author's record-setting two-handed Round-Australia race with Mike Quilter. *Photo: Group Kiwi.*

Below: Computer graphics aid the helmsman and cockpit crew aboard *Steinlager 2*. Racing or cruising, when it comes to sailing instruments, only the best are good enough. *Photo: Group Kiwi.*

struggling with poorly-designed or malfunctioning instruments.

I believe the following are essential for peak performance on a modern racing keeler:

• Wind direction indicator (close-hauled or digital 360 degrees).
• Digital wind speed indicator.
• Boat speed indicator (preferably digital in 1/100th of a knot graduations).
• Echo-sounder with cockpit readout. This allows you to sail as close to shore as possible to avoid an unfavourable tide. Make sure you know at what depth the keel touches bottom and mark the readout accordingly.

The gun goes for the start of New Zealand's annual Coastal Classic Race and the fleet breaks away in search of clear air and the good start essential to any race-winning strategy. *Photo: Group Kiwi.*

Summary

• Know the racing rules.
• Be a punctual, considerate and keen crew member.
• Proper pre-race boat preparation can help win races.
• Know how to select the right sail materials and racing instruments.

Chapter 8

RACE-WINNING
TACTICS

EVERY racing sailor has his or her own ideas on tactics, a subject discussed endlessly in yacht-club bars throughout the world.

A good start

In the previous chapter I touched briefly on what preparations a racing skipper and crew might make, and mentioned the importance of a good start. I make no apologies for stressing yet again the need for start-line discipline. I like to be in the vicinity of the line at least an hour before the start. This gives the crew time to settle down. The cook makes a hot brew, and sweet biscuits are handed round while we go through a crew chat, plan tactics, confirm crew positions and discuss

the opposition. If the race is a long one, watches are confirmed and finally we run through a few timed starts, look at the lay of the line, check what the tide is doing, where the wind-shifts may be and what headsails and spinnakers we are likely to need.

Within the starting period it is important that the crew remain quiet and concentrate on their particular job, ignoring distractions on competing or spectator craft wherever possible. A good lookout should be kept, preferably a bow-man if the vessel is big enough, and the navigator should give a timed countdown audible to all the crew.

Don't stray too far from the line. If the wind

is variable, you can leave the choice of headsails until the 10-minute gun — but no later, as it may affect your start. Keep an eye on the opposition. Don't try to beat much bigger yachts but keep as clear of them as possible. Clear wind is as important as being in the right place.

At the start gun it is best to be going fast (if in a big fleet) so as to reach clear air as quickly as possible. Get the crew to settle down to their respective jobs, still with no more chat than is necessary, and if the first mark is only a couple of miles away, the navigator should have worked out the next course and be calculating the apparent wind speed and direction after the mark.

Keep any further food and drink away from the

Left: An alert lookout, preferably at the bow, is essential for big-fleet starts. *Photo: Group Kiwi.*

Below: A Soling-class massed start. In a big fleet like this, it's best to be going fast at the gun in order to reach clean air as quickly as possible. *Photo: Roger Lean-Vercoe.*

crew until you are in a very settled leg of the course. Even then, the crew should not all eat together. Sandwiches can be handed round, but not to the trimmers or helmsman, who should be relieved of their positions before eating.

Keep 'em covered

The most important post-start lesson I have learned from a career which has included five Whitbread Round the World Races, is *always cover the opposition*. It doesn't matter whether the race is around the buoys or around the world, the lesson applies. Don't take a flyer unless you are so far behind that it is your only hope of catching up. Flyers can pay, but rarely do.

Always keep between the opposition and the mark, whether it is two or 5000 miles away.

The navigator should pre-draw the race course on to a chart and keep a check on the yacht's position during the beat. Unless there is a known advantage to be gained from going outside the tacking cone (Fig. 9), don't. If the wind shifts you could overlay the mark and let boats inside but behind you get there first. Keeping inside the cone is the safe way to go.

In a big and competitive fleet, try to end up coming to a windward mark on starboard tack; don't underlay the mark at all on the last tack. If there are other boats around you, the wind will be very disturbed and trying to pinch up on starboard to get round the mark will almost certainly cost you more ground than if you had continued slightly on the previous tack to make the last one an easy lay.

Heading from a windward to a leeward mark, try to keep within a reasonable distance of the course between the two marks. End up in a luffing match and you may find yourself way off to one side of the track and having let others through. Not good. Again, the cone is a reliable guide.

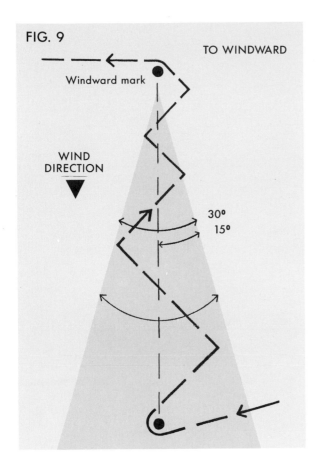

FIG. 9

TO WINDWARD

Windward mark

WIND
DIRECTION

30°
15°

Above left: Rod Davis keeps between his opposition and the mark for a decisive match-race lead against World Champion Russell Coutts. *Photo: Group Kiwi.*

Above right: This Fireball pair know the advantage to be gained in a big fleet by approaching the windward mark on starboard tack and so avoiding the need to pinch up in disturbed air around the buoy. *Photo: Roger Lean-Vercoe.*

On any part of the track try to keep in as clear and undisturbed air as possible. Even experienced skippers often fail to realise how great the distance is over which disturbed air from one boat will affect another, and if the start-line is jammed with yachts it oftens pays to take the 'wrong' end just to be in clear air.

The role of the navigator/tactician must never be underestimated. For example, on a broad reach with the wind at 100 degrees apparent and the mark coming up, the next leg looks like a reach ... but will you be able to carry a spinnaker? If so, which one? The navigator should have worked out the strength and direction of the new apparent wind before the mark is reached and in time for the crew to prepare the next sail, i.e., spinnaker, genoa or whatever. It may mean a reef in the mainsail, the spinnaker dropped and the No. 3 genoa hoisted. All this takes time and huge gains can be made here from a correct calculation by the navigator/tactician.

Using your polars

Throughout tuning and racing, the navigator should keep notes from which a **polar table** or diagram (often abbreviated to 'polar') can be drawn. This is a graphic representation of the speed of which the yacht is capable on different points of sail, in different wind and sea conditions, and under different sail configurations (Fig. 10).

Depending on the degree of electronic sophistication you can afford and/or on how seriously you approach your racing, it may be worthwhile investing in an on-board computer and suitable software for preparation of your vessel's polars. The overwhelming advantage of computerisation is that polars can be continuously and instantly updated and even, at the most advanced level, integrated for direct input from the vessel's navigational and monitoring instruments. Let's look at a basic example of how to use your polars.

1. Assuming a wind of 20 knots apparent at 90 degrees apparent, then according to the polar graph the yacht should be sailing at, say, 7.62 knots with a flanker spinnaker, small staysail and flattened-off mainsail. If it is not reaching this speed, something is wrong with the trim. Work at it until the speed is reached and if an even higher speed is reached, the navigator should amend the polar accordingly so that next time you will be trying for the higher figure.

2. You are sailing to windward with 25 knots of apparent wind at 30 degrees apparent angle. According to your polar, under No. 3 genoa and with one reef in the mainsail, you should be getting, say, 6.9 knots in a choppy sea. You will maybe have already tried a No. 2 and two reefs earlier in the season and found that you get only 6.8 knots at 30 degrees apparent in the same wind and sea conditions. But is 30 degrees apparent wind angle the best to be sailing at to achieve maximum VMG (Velocity Made Good) towards the windward mark? Maybe it is better to sail at 32 degrees apparent at higher speed or 28 degrees apparent at lower speed?

The navigator should have solved such tactical

Sheer muscle power can be useful . . . but if you're serious about racing it pays to add a computer, too! *Photo: Roger Lean-Vercoe.*

FIG. 10 Polar tables

Apparent wind speed (knots)	Apparent wind angle (degrees)							
	30	40	50	60	70	80	90	100
	BOAT SPEED — KNOTS							
5		2.8	3.2	3.5	3.6	3.7	3.7	3.7
10	4.0	5.1	5.2	5.3	5.5	5.8	6.0	6.0
15	6.2	7.5	7.6	7.7	7.7	7.8	7.8	7.8
20	6.3	7.6	7.7	7.8	7.8	7.8	7.8	7.9
25	6.1	7.3	7.5	7.6	7.6	7.7	8.0	8.0

Apparent wind speed (knots)								
	110	120	130	140	150	160	170	180
	BOAT SPEED — KNOTS							
5	3.6	3.5	3.3	3.0	3.0	3.0	2.9	2.8
10	5.9	5.9	5.6	5.7	5.5	5.5	5.5	5.4
15	7.9	8.0	7.8	7.8	7.8	7.8	7.8	7.7
20	8.0	8.0	8.0	8.0	8.1	8.0	7.9	
25	8.1	8.2	SURFING					

dilemmas as these or, alternatively, your Brookes and Gatehouse Hercules will offer an automatic readout so the helmsman knows he is sailing at the right wind angle and speed.

The advantage of polars and the VMG predictions are that they save so much guesswork. In the middle of the night when the wind has increased, rather than the crew having a discussion on which sails to use, it is a simple matter to refer to the polar diagram. When the sail change is made, you'll know what speed you should be getting rather than just thinking you are going well because of all the noise and spray.

Layers and shear

There are a couple of situations in which polars may be unreliable and they arise when the wind is *layered* or has *a high shear factor*. A layered wind is faster at the masthead than at deck level. Obviously this is more noticeable on larger yachts and the effect is that although the wind-speed indicator is registering 25 knots apparent, the yacht feels undercanvassed with the No. 3 genoa and one reef in the mainsail dictated by its polars. Because the vessel is sailing in different wind-speed 'layers,' the reading is false and it may perform better with, say, the No. 1 genoa.

While 'layering' relates to wind speeds that vary according to the height above sea level, 'shear' is when the wind varies in direction at different heights. Occasionally the luffs of the sails will lift at different wind angles on opposite tacks when sailing to windward. I have been sailing with the masthead indicator showing the wind from straight ahead on one tack and from the beam on the other. Similarly the sails lifted at the bottom on one tack at the same time as they were full at the top. On the opposite tack they were full at the bottom and flapping up high. This doesn't happen often, but it's worth being aware of. The wind up high is going in a different direction to that close to the surface of the sea. This is wind shear.

Above: Tracy Edwards and crew prepare for a sail change aboard their round-the-world racer, *Maiden*. Photo: Roger Lean-Vercoe.

Right: All the excitement of keelboat racing shows in this dramatic photograph of a nail-biting incident as two competitors on starboard tack narrowly avoid an opponent (KA303) on port. Photo: Roger Lean-Vercoe.

Sail selection

Finally, on the question of tactical sail selection: remember that warmer tropical winds comprise air less dense than in colder climates, so while you may start your ocean race in fresh conditions under only a No. 3 jib and with one reef in the mainsail, if your route takes you closer to the Equator, e.g., the Whangarei (New Zealand) to Noumea (New Caledonia) Race, you may find that towards the finish line the yacht performs better in the same wind strength carrying a No. 2 genoa and full main. The wind speed is the same but it is warmer and less dense.

"Bear away, you're over the line!" Confusion at the start of a McNamara Bowl race as several of the fleet, going flat out, jump the gun. *Photo: Roger Lean-Vercoe.*

Summary
- Start-line discipline is the first essential.
- Always keep the opposition covered.
- Stay in clear air as much as possible.
- Maintain your polar tables.
- Sail changes can be dictated by local conditions.

Chapter 9

MAINTENANCE CAN BE FUN

THE OLD JOKE that sailboats are holes in the water into which people pour money seems only too true when you are adding up the bills for insurance premiums, mooring and marina fees, hauling-out charges, gear repair and replacement. Fortunately, the owner prepared to tackle his or her own maintenance can reduce the amount of money going down that hole. Looking after your boat is more than just saving money, however. It can be fun, and many owners gain as much pleasure and relaxation from a weekend 'working on the boat' as from actually sailing it. In this chapter we'll look at some of the systems and methods I have used over many years of owning

sailboats to ensure that everything functions efficiently and lasts as long as possible. Once again we'll divide the boat into its major components.

The hull

As indicated in Chapters 4 and 6, while fibreglass hulls require less frequent attention than wood or steel, they are not totally maintenance-free as is sometimes claimed. A good fibreglass hull should last 5–10 years from new (depending on the level of ultra-violet light to which it is exposed) without needing repainting. During that time, a regular polish to restore the shine is all that should be necessary. Make sure you use a

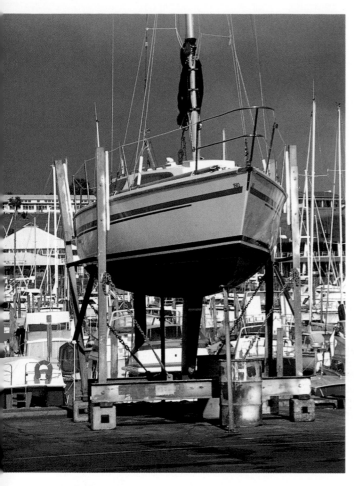

Left: A good fibreglass hull such as this should last 5–10 years without needing repainting, but regular haulouts, scrubbing and polishing are necessary to keep marine growth at bay and maintain the hull's good looks and efficiency. *Photo: Group Kiwi.*

Right: Looking after your boat is more than just saving money — many owners gain as much pleasure from 'working on the boat' as from actually sailing it. *Photo: Group Kiwi.*

polish recommended by a boat-paint specialist. Silicone-based car or domestic polishes can cause problems when it comes to repainting.

Each time your boat is out of the water (at least once a year), check for signs of osmosis, which will show up as blisters and/or roughening of the hull surface. Today's fibreglass boatbuilders use vinylester resins which greatly reduce the risk of osmosis, but most hulls moulded in the '70s and '80s contain polyester resins and it has been estimated that 70 per cent have suffered some degree of osmosis. Treated in time, it can be relatively easily eradicated; left unchecked, it will spread and eventually mean the cutting out and replacing of large areas of hull — if not a complete new moulding.

A blister or two does not, of course, mean the hull has osmosis. It is often simple paint-surface blistering — but if in doubt, seek advice.

Fibreglass slowly degrades when exposed to sunlight, becoming chalky and/or dull. The surface may start to craze and no amount of polishing will restore the shine. At this point it's time to start work with the cleaning fluid, rubbing papers (silicone carbide for fibreglass), paint rollers and brushes. You may also need a fibreglass repair kit to make good any small cracks, scratches or nicks.

Marine-paint manufacturers offer several types of paint suitable for fibreglass (mostly polyurethane-based) and, of course, you will need a good anti-fouling below the waterline. If you know what brand and type of paint was previously used on your boat, it's probably best to stick with the same system. In any case, read the paint manufacturer's instructions carefully before buying. With marine paints more than any other you must follow these instructions to the

letter, otherwise you'll spend a lot of time and money only to have paint peeling off almost before you are back on the water.

Timber hulls need regular repainting (preferably once a year) and a lot of preparatory work. They also need to be dry, so allow ample drying-off time between hauling out and paint application. To check whether any dampness remains, dust any suspect areas with French chalk or talcum powder, leave for a couple of hours and if the powder has darkened in colour, the timber is still wet.

You must sand down (or water-blast) the hull to remove all marine growth, salt, dirt, oil, grease, etc. Use good quality aluminium oxide or silicone carbide paper and if re-coating an existing system, make sure remaining patches of paint are sanded to a matt finish. Fill any nail holes, chips, etc., and sand smooth.

Before any paint is applied, oily timbers such as teak should be wiped all over with clean rags soaked in methylene chloride.

In hot, sunny weather, apply the first coat of primer as soon as possible after preparation is complete, or cover the hull to prevent it over-drying in direct sunlight. Timber-planking can open up if exposed to the sun for too long. For a good, lasting finish you'll need a primer, two undercoats and two finish coats topsides, with anti-fouling replacing the finish coats below the waterline. The paint manufacturer's instructions will include a covering rate, and a rough guide to the area of your hull can be gained from the following formula:

Topsides: LOA + draft × 2

Below the waterline: LWL (waterline length) × (beam + draft). Reduce by 50 per cent for racing-type fin keelers, 25 per cent for long, cruising-type keels.

Steel hulls require regular attention because once rust takes hold it is extremely difficult to remove by physical means (wire brushing, sanding, sand-blasting, etc.). A neutralising acid (usually phosphoric acid) after thorough wire-brushing or sand-blasting is the only reliable treatment for rust prior to repainting.

The hull will need to be thoroughly washed with fresh water and any loose or flaky paint removed. Remaining gloss paint must be sanded to a matt finish. As with wood, you'll need a primer coat, two undercoats and two top (or anti-fouling) coats for a satisfactory job.

Aluminium is tricky because it tends to be greasy and needs to be thoroughly wiped down with cleaning fluid before painting or repainting. A previously unpainted surface will also require sand-blasting (or grinding) and acid etching. Two primer coats, two undercoats and two finish coats are recommended.

Sails

Dacron is particularly prone to mildew and if your boat has been laid up for winter and/or not used for several months, remove all sails and spread then out on a lawn to air. Check seams and batten pockets for damaged stitching, and you may need to re-lash the slides on the luff and foot of the mainsail. If the sails have bolt-ropes, make sure they are not coming away at the headboard or clew. Areas of chafe should be repaired by a sailmaker.

Headsail hanks (particularly on storm jibs) tend to corrode, the plungers sticking either open or closed. A squirt of WD40 and some working up and down before wiping off the excess with a clean rag will solve the problem.

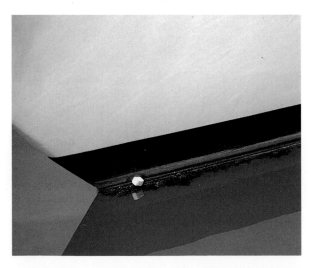

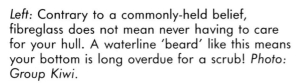

Left: Contrary to a commonly-held belief, fibreglass does not mean never having to care for your hull. A waterline 'beard' like this means your bottom is long overdue for a scrub! *Photo: Group Kiwi.*

Top: Wheel-operated steering systems need careful attention and should be thoroughly checked at least once a year. Cordage *(above left)* suffers badly from chafe and must be replaced when, as here, it shows signs of excessive wear and strands are starting to break. *Above right:* A good wash-down and a squirt of WD40 is often enough for the mainsheet car, but if the sheaves will not turn easily it may need to be dismantled and cleared of caked salt, etc. *Photos: Group Kiwi.*

Salty and/or damp sails should be washed in fresh water. Those on a yacht of up to about 12m (40ft) will usually fit in the bath, but you'll need a hose for anything bigger. Make sure the sails (particularly the reinforced corners) are bone-dry before re-bagging.

Spars (mast, boom, etc.)

Remove and grease any squeaky sheaves. (Spraying with WD40 is a good temporary measure.) Potential troublemakers include halyard sheaves, exit boxes and slots, spinnaker halyard blocks and screw fastenings. Look for loose screws and signs of corrosion or chafe.

Once a year wipe the mast (particularly the spreaders) with a cleaning agent to help prevent sails becoming dirty and marked. A varnished or painted mast must have any scratches or other damage touched up to ensure the integrity of the protective paint.

If any pins are covered with anti-chafe tape, remove the tape and check. Never reuse split pins or seizing wire; reuse can lead to a major rig failure.

Every few years the mast should be taken out for a full strip-down, check and overhaul.

Standing rigging

If stainless steel, a visual inspection and wipe with a kerosene (paraffin)-dampened rag should be enough. Re-grease rigging screws — but before loosening, mark the threads with insulating tape so that the screw can be retightened to the same position. Shackles should be moused, i.e., bound with wire or twine across the open end to prevent accidental releasing, and split-pins covered by rigging tape or anti-chafe material.

Aloft in a bosun's chair, check for broken wire strands. Badly rusted wire should be replaced immediately, minor rusting removed with a wire brush followed by a coat of Fisholene or varnish.

Rod rigging should be cleaned with a kerosene-soaked rag and checked carefully, especially the fittings. Discolouration can hide fatigue cracks. Treat rigging screws as for stainless-steel wire.

Running rigging (halyards)

Rope-to-wire splices should be neat and free from sprags; use a sharp knife to remove them. The wire should also be free from sprags, stainless steel being more vulnerable than galvanised. The rope tail should be in good order and whipped at the bitter end. The talurit or splice connecting the wire halyard to the clips should look OK. If chewed-up or messy, replace it. (In most cases re-termination is satisfactory.) Otherwise, just tape over. The clip should open easily and any shackles should be moused to prevent the pin falling out.

Hydraulics

Check for leaks and trace the piping from reservoir to cylinders for signs of chafe or wear. Wipe the cylinders with a detergent and soft cloth. Check the reservoir oil level and make sure your have spare oil on board because it is often hard to get the right grade, especially in out-of-the-way places.

Deck gear

A thorough hose-down followed by a squirt of WD40 should take care of the blocks. If the mainsheet car is of the roller-bearing type, remove any caked salt, soak in warm water and detergent and scrub with a stiff brush. Spray with WD40 before replacing on the track. If the block and cars are salt-encrusted, the sheaves will not turn easily, friction will increase, along with the effort needed to pull in a sail or alter the position of the mainsheet traveller.

Lifelines, pushpit and pulpit

Metal polish and a soft cloth will care for stainless steel. Check that stanchion bases are still securely bolted through the deck and showing no sign of movement. Lifelines must be tight. Check the shackles, lashings and bottle-screws at the ends for security and renew if in any doubt.

Lashings should be sewn in place, otherwise they tend to come undone. Cover all securing bolts, split-pins and sharp corners with pieces of leather or tape. A split-pin sticking out can mean a sore foot for someone, to say nothing of ruined deck-shoes and/or sails.

Anchors, chain and warps

Whatever type of anchor you use (and I like the CQR for general use), it must always be in good condition. If showing signs of rust, have it re-galvanised. (In a CQR that will mean replacing the lead in the point as it will melt in the process.)

The anchor chain should be reasonably free of rust and marked with white paint at regular intervals: one band = 10m, two bands = 20m, three bands = 30m, and so on. Anchor warps should be of the non-floating type, nylon being best as it stretches under load. Warps should be tagged (marked) as for chain but using coloured material sewn into the lay of the rope. It is vitally important that you know the amount of warp let out when anchoring if you are to avoid dragging. Without marks you can only guess.

It pays to end-for-end the chain and warp every couple of seasons, i.e., turn them around to even up the wear.

Electrics

Lightly spray the electrical panel with water-repellent. Check the acid level in the battery (batteries) and top up with distilled water. Terminals should be clean and lightly smeared with petroleum jelly. Wipe the top of the battery and make sure it is firmly clamped and not likely to come adrift in a knock-down or roll. It will preferably be in an acid-proof box.

Below left: Check all lifelines and stanchions, particularly that the bases are secure, and make sure all navigational lights are working. *Photo: Group Kiwi.*

Below right: Wooden hulls need a lot of TLC, i.e., cleaning, scraping and repainting, preferably once a year. *Photo: Group Kiwi.*

Navigation/mast lights

These *must* work! It is worth taking out the bulbs, cleaning them and smearing the metal connecting ends lightly with petroleum jelly. Have spare bulbs aboard and make sure they work. Do the emergency (dry-cell) navigation lights operate? Where are they stowed? Find them, check the batteries and make sure they are in order.

Thoroughly check all radio equipment and test it by calling up the local marine station.

Better-quality sailing instruments have dessicators built into the control boxes and repeater dials. These should be removed and dried out if necessary. Read the instruction booklet if in doubt.

Examine all electrical connections, especially those on deck, as poor connections are the most frequent cause of failure. Clean and re-terminate if necessary and use the water-repellent spray before re-installing a repeater.

Compass light

The compass light has been the most unreliable and poorly-made fitting on every boat I have sailed. Corrosion sets in at an extraordinary rate around the bulb-holder, so check carefully, clean and replace. If in doubt, fit a new bulb, painted with red nail varnish if not pre-coloured. (Red lighting in a compass is best for night vision).

Engine

Sump oil fuel and oil filters need changing every six months. Clean or replace the water-inlet filter gauze (turning off the inlet valve first if the boat is in the water).

If the gearbox is hydraulic, check the oil level. The stuffing box where the propeller shaft exits from the hull may need attention or just a turn of the grease-cap. When correctly adjusted, the stern gland will become only warm and no more than an occasional drop of water will enter while the shaft is turning at normal revs. If it runs hot, loosen the gland-nut a little; if water pours in, tighten it a little.

Look over all electrical connections to the engine, cleaning and spraying lightly with WD40. Keep the engine generally clean and if you are not likely to be running it for several months, squirt a fair amount of WD40 into the air intake. Close off the exhaust outlet and water inlet valves, then lightly spray the engine (particularly the electrical connections) with WD40. This done, and with the battery in good condition, the engine should start readily next time you need it.

If the starter battery is low, a few turns of the crank handle before trying to start it electrically will loosen things up and pull less power from the battery.

Don't forget the controls, i.e., throttle cables and gear-shift levers/cables. If using Morse-type, single-lever controls in the cockpit, take the unit apart and examine the workings. Clean and lubricate before reassembling. While I was docking *Condor of Bermuda* at the end of the 1979 Sydney–Hobart race, the gear-control unit in the cockpit exploded and only a tyre conveniently overhanging the wall where we hit prevented what could have been serious hull damage.

Look for loose bolts and hose-clips on the engine itself. If there is oil in the sump tray, ask yourself why. If water drips from a fitting, something is not right. Most problems start in a minor way but develop quickly unless corrected in time.

Engine-mounting bolts are important. They must be tight, with lock-nuts for added security. We could have had a life-threatening disaster aboard the 1981-82 Whitbread entry, *Ceramco New Zealand*, had we not discovered, en route to the start, that only one nut remained on the engine-mounting feet. No lock-nuts had been fitted.

Outboard motors

Outboard engines should be run in fresh water a couple of times a year to rid the cooling system of salt. Discard fuel mixture more than a year old. Remove the plugs (using the correct tool), clean and reset the gap. Replace if the ceramic insulator

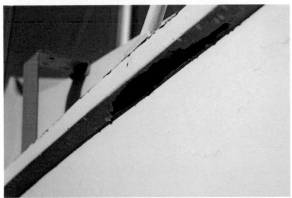

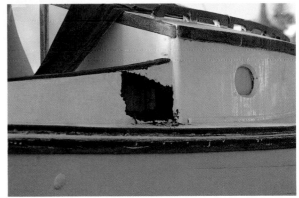

Top: Sadly neglected and ill-used, this anchor chain has rusted beyond the point of safety and should be replaced. *Photo: Group Kiwi.*

Above left and right: A little gentle probing with a screwdriver or file during the annual maintenance check can often have surprising (and alarming) results. *Photos: Group Kiwi.*

is cracked or broken. Every moving part not in its own casing should be given a regular spray with WD40 or light oil. Some moving parts will have grease nipples. Check the state of the grease in the grease-box near the propeller and replace if there are signs of contamination.

Finally, with all engines, petrol or diesel, inboard or outboard, do refer to the manual and adhere to its recommended oil/filter change schedules. Keep a note in your log of the hours run.

Pumps

Diaphragm-type bilge pumps should be opened and hair, matchsticks, soggy paper labels, or whatever, removed. When reassembling, lightly smear flaps and seals with petroleum jelly, then make sure the pump still works!

Galley

Once a year — more if necessary — the stove should be stripped down and cleaned. Watch for food scraps near the gas jets at the back of the oven; they are almost impossible to reach unless the unit is taken apart. Valves should be lubricated and worn jets replaced before reassembly.

Safety equipment

Once a year check the expiry date on fire extinguishers and flares. If a fire extinguisher has been used it should be properly serviced. It should also be mounted in an accessible place. Never stow fire extinguishers in lockers or under bunks. If you need one, you'll need it in a hurry.

Check the general exterior condition of all liferafts and take for re-service if the expiry date is near.

The inflatable dinghy should be checked, washed and dried.

Every lifejacket should have a whistle attached

Above and right: All hands to the winches . . . ocean racing crews work their deck gear hard, and racing winches need regular and careful servicing if they are to cope with the tremendous loads imposed on them. *Photos: Roger Lean-Vercoe.*

and all clips, buckles, etc., should be free and easy to operate. Lubricate if metal.

Wash safety harnesses and pay particular attention to the clips, spraying lightly with WD40. Check safety lines for chafe and webbing for broken stitches.

Depending on where you sail, minimum flare requirements vary. For ocean work, always carry Category One as standard. Replace out-of-date flares (normally three years after manufacture).

Emergency torches are part of your safety equipment. Make sure the batteries are not starting to corrode or leak. Check terminals and bulb-holders.

Cordage

Modern ropes need little attention, but I recommend whipping rather than taping the ends. On a cruising boat a yearly wash in fresh water should be good enough for all cordage, but the serious racing owner will give them a good hose-off after every race. Washing shifts salt crystals which can cut into fibres.

Chafe is the only other major problem — and that usually only on long voyages. A sheet can wear through in a night if rubbing on a stanchion or guardrail, so always keep a few lengths of plastic hose handy to tie onto the rope to protect it from chafing. A bag of sheepskin will also pay for itself on a long trip. When mooring to the dockside or marina, it pays to have a good anti-chafe system; soft plastic tubing is as good as any.

Steering system

A tiller and rudder need little more than painting, especially if transom-hung. An inboard rudder may need greasing. Wheel-operated systems are a different matter and it pays to go over them carefully. If of the wire-and-chain type, clean and grease the chain sprockets and all bearings. Check the wire for sprags and renew if any are found. If the system is of the gearbox-and-shaft type, the gearboxes should be checked once a year to ensure that they are still full of grease. Lubricate all universal joints with a grease-gun and check any bearings for 'sloppiness'.

Wheel systems should have an emergency tiller. Make sure you know where it is and how it works.

If the vessel has hydraulic steering, go over it carefully for signs of leakage. Lubricate nipples on the actuator arm with a grease-gun.

Winches

Racing winches need regular servicing. Use WD40 or a light machine oil if tailing at speed on sophisticated winches. The lubrication won't stand up to weeks at sea and mooring through the winter. It washes off. For long-distance racing or cruising I always use a good quality readily available water-resistant grease such as BP Ener-grease. It is ideal for winches, steering glands, rudder shafts and rigging screws.

Propeller

When the boat is out of the water, or even alongside a pile for a scrub-off, check the state of the propeller and that there are no signs of electrolytic corrosion. The sacrificial zinc block on the shaft must be in good condition and firmly clamped. If badly worn, waste no time replacing it or you'll soon find yourself up for a new propeller.

Ventilation

The need for good ventilation cannot be over-stressed. Apart from keeping the downstairs free of mould and sweet smelling, it hinders rot and is the best possible guard against seasickness. For the record, about 0.42cu.m (15cu.ft) of fresh air per minute is the minimum required for each person on board. Watch the burners on your stove — if the flame is orange instead of blue, you are low on oxygen.

Dodgers which allow hatches and ports to remain open in most weather conditions are admirable, as are dorade-type ventilators. Dorade vents should have a cord attached to stop them going overboard should a large wave come aboard or a flapping sheet rip one off.

Going back to the 15cu.ft of air required by each person aboard, it's worth noting that a 102-mm (4-in.) diameter dorade vent or cowl will take in 0.33cu.m (12cu.ft) of air a minute in 4 knots of wind; in the same wind speed a 127-mm (5-in.) diameter vent or cowl will admit 0.59cu.m (21cu.ft) a minute.

When the vessel is left on a mooring, as many ventilators as possible should be in place, even if not used while sailing. Open some lockers to allow air to circulate and if sails are damp, don't store them in sailbags but lay them through the boat to dry out while you are away.

Wet-weather clothing

Wash in warm, soapy water and dry thoroughly — a procedure rarely followed but which extends the life of wet-weather gear. Hang up any gear left aboard — don't stuff it in the nearest locker. Every

Left: Check all rigging regularly, looking for broken wire strands, rust, discolouration and other danger signs. Where necessary, wrap on plenty of anti-chafe material and secure with rigging tape. *Photo: Group Kiwi.*

Below: Look for signs of electrolytic corrosion on the propeller and sacrificial zinc block. If the latter appears to be badly worn, don't hesitate to replace it. *Photo: Group Kiwi.*

now and then lubricate the zips with a dry lubricant of the type sold in dive shops. If any item of gear has a hole, take it back to the manufacturer. Most have a repair service that costs a lot less than new gear.

A regular maintenance routine pays off

As will be seen from the above, maintenance is very much a matter of commonsense and attention to detail. A boat and its gear comprise many different types of material, each of which requires a specific method of cleaning and protection against the ravages of salt, mildew, micro-organisms, fungii, rain, dust, ultra-violet light, general wear and tear, and neglect. Working through a regular maintenance programme is a chore, but one you won't regret. The alternative could be a 'funny burning smell', grating noise or a spreading pool of oil suddenly becoming apparent when you are 30 km (20 miles) offshore, short-handed and struggling with 35 knots of wind and a seasick family!

Hauling out and working through a regular maintenance programme might seem a chore, but for many boat owners it can be almost as rewarding as sailing itself. And like sailing, much of what needs to be done is just plain commonsense. *Photo: Group Kiwi.*

Summary

- Even fibreglass hulls need regular maintenance.
- Choose the right paint system and follow the instructions for use.
- Chafe, salt, mildew . . . sails need a lot of care, too.
- Varnish, oil and grease for all standing rigging.
- Check out those rope-to-wire splices and mouse all shackles.
- Deck gear, lifelines, ground tackle, all suffer from salt.
- Navigation lights **MUST** work!
- Regularly check safety equipment expiry dates.
- Good below-deck ventilation cannot be over-stressed.

Chapter 10

THE ART OF
NAVIGATION

NAVIGATION is often called 'the black art', but while it is essential in some form or other for any boat trip, be it across the harbour or around the world, like so many things relating to the sea, it is really far less frightening than it appears to be.

In the following chapter we can touch only briefly on the subject, but Ross Norgrove, a veteran cruising and charter skipper, wrote in his book *The Cruising Life:* 'To the neophyte, one of the most fearsome aspects of sailing is the art of navigation. It needn't be so. Determining a ship's position and plotting it on a chart nowadays demands only the ability to add two and two.'

Since that was written, the advent of advanced navigational systems such as GPS (Global Positioning Satellite) has removed even the need to add two and two. Press a button and, hey presto, a little box tells you exactly where you are. As with everything, however, there is always a nagging 'but ...'. In the case of electronic navigational aids such as Satnav and GPS, it must be 'but what happens if the boat runs out of power?' Indeed, at least one extensive ocean search-and-rescue operation has been mounted for a cruising yacht on which just that happened: the batteries and generator were swamped in heavy

seas, the boat lost the use of its radio and navigational instruments — and no one aboard had a clue about how to use the sextant, compass and navigation tables.

Basic navigational 'tools'

With modern satellite communications, a vast array of on-board equipment is available to the navigator, limited only by what the boat's owner can afford, but some basic 'tools' should still be aboard every yacht that ventures beyond harbour limits — and someone should know how to use them. They include:

• A barometer (check the reading and adjust every few months).
• Binoculars (max 7 x 50).
• A pair of good-quality single-handed dividers.
• Parallel rules or equivalent (I prefer the roller type).
• Hand-bearing compass with illumination for

night use (the best you can afford).
• Radio receiver (AM and marine band).
• Log book (a ruled exercise book will do).
• A properly-swung and corrected steering compass with deviation card.
• Charts of the area in which the boat operates.

For the long-distance cruiser add the following to the list:

• SSB transceiver.
• Sextant (two if possible, one as a back-up).
• Radio direction-finder (RDF).
• An accurate timepiece (digital watches are extremely accurate).
• Appropriate tide tables, *Sight Reduction Tables for AIR Navigation* (or equivalent), appropriate *Pilots*.

I also like to carry Mary Blewitt's two books, *Navigation for Yachtsmen* and *Celestial Navigation for Yachtsmen*, probably the most widely used and recommended by navigators around the world.

Once you have the above, can find your way around the coast, use a sextant proficiently and know what to do with the information it provides, you can then start thinking about the more advanced aids.

The radio direction-finder is particularly useful. It comprises a radio-receiver fitted with a highly directional aerial. The best makes also have a built-in compass so that it is possible to tune the radio to the correct frequency, then point the unit in the direction you think the signal beacon should be. The point of 'null' (no signal), is the bearing, which can then be read directly off the compass mounted on the receiver. The bearing can then be transferred to the chart. Simple — but it takes practice, and there are a few pitfalls. I never use RDF more than 50 miles from a beacon: at dusk and at dawn I also leave it in its locker.

Words like 'sextant' and 'Sight Reduction Tables' invite looks of horror from many people, the usual reaction being that unless you are extremely good at maths, finding your position

Left: Even out for a relaxing harbour sail aboard *Steinlager 2*, the author keeps a navigator's expert eye on the maxi's computer screen and sailing instruments. *Photo: Group Kiwi.*

Below: Radar dome, radio antennae and other navigational aids are clearly visible above the stern of Florence Arthaud's high-tech racing trimaran *Pierre 1er*. *Photo: Roger Lean-Vercoe.*

at sea from the sun, moon, planets and stars is far too difficult. However, practice and patience are the only attributes needed beyond the ability to add, subtract and tell the time.

Go through the sight-taking routine step by step several times and all will become clear. You probably won't understand how it works, but it doesn't matter. Once you can use the sextant, the black art will shade to grey and, with practice, eventually become no more to be feared than finding your way around the city streets. My first exercise in celestial navigation consisted of finding the position of our house with the aid of a bucket of water on the front lawn, and ever since then I have enjoyed the tremendous feeling of satisfaction that comes from correct navigation, even at its simplest levels.

For the club-racing skipper, too, whose budget is unlikely to stretch to Satnav and GPS, basic navigation can mean the difference between finishing first or in the middle of the fleet; for his cruising counterpart a few minutes at the chart table before setting off can save a lot of time and worry.

Peter Blake aboard the 26-m catamaran *ENZA* in which he and Britain's Robin Knox-Johnston attempted to win the Jules Verne Trophy by rounding the world in less than 80 days. Their effort came to an end when *ENZA* struck an unidentified floating object in the Southern Ocean and, with the starboard hull badly damaged, was forced to return to Cape Town for repairs. The trophy went to rival French catamaran *Commodore Explorer*, skippered by Bruno Peyron, which completed the 28,000 nautical mile journey in 79 days 6 hours 15 minutes and 56 seconds. *Photo: Pickthall Picture Library.*

Summary

•   Don't be frightened . . . navigation can be fun.
•   Electronics like Satnav and GPS make it easy . . . but what happens when the power fails?
•   Learn to use the basic tools, from compass and chart to sextant.
•   If cruising or racing offshore do take a course in navigation, or at least carefully study a specialist book on the subject; and practise until perfect!

INDEX